BRITISH RAILWAYS IN COLOUR
1948-1968
A Period of Transition

The last few years of express passenger workings on the S&D line witnessed the use of BR '9F' 2-10-0s unaided on the heaviest trains. In August 1962, No 92245 pauses at adverse signals at Templecombe with a southbound holiday special. Colour-Rail SD128/J. G. Dewing

Below:
A Class 45 'Peak' locomotive at Ferryhill on the East Coast main line with train 1V96, the 15.15 Newcastle-Bristol, on 12 May 1968. John M. Boyes

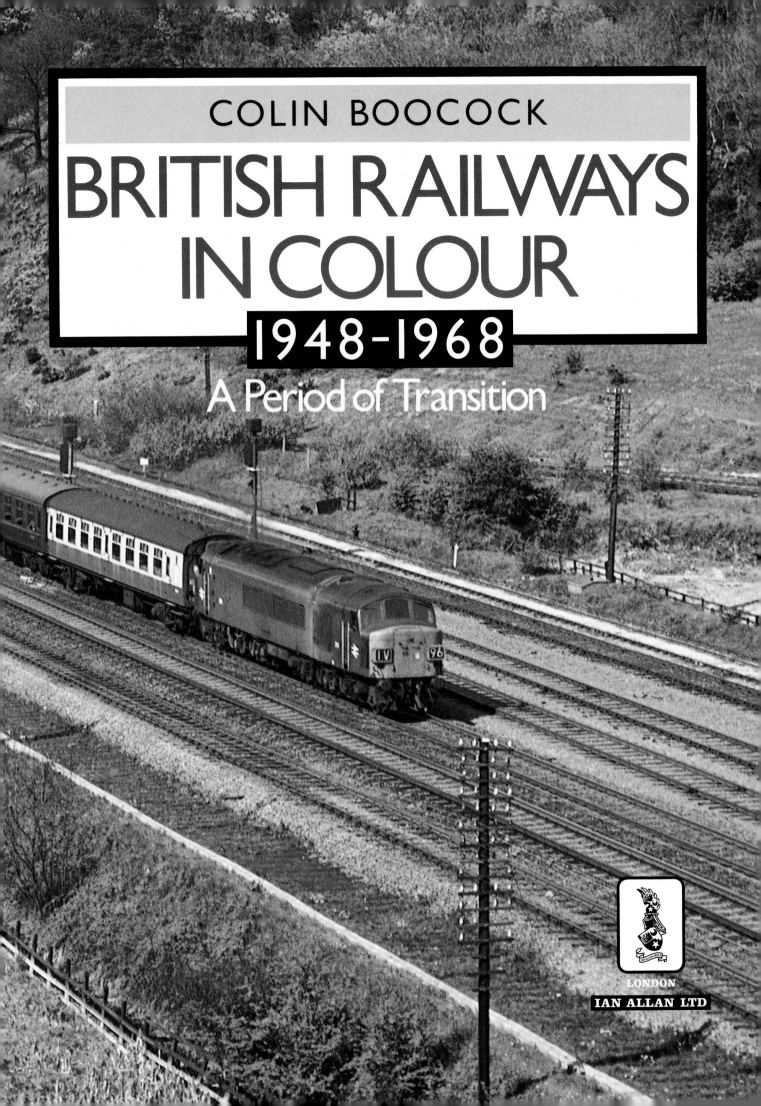

COLIN BOOCOCK

BRITISH RAILWAYS IN COLOUR

1948-1968

A Period of Transition

LONDON

IAN ALLAN LTD

Dedication
This book is dedicated to Jack Turner.

Acknowledgements
This book benefits greatly from the wide range of colour transparencies made available to the enthusiast public by Colour-Rail. The selection is really vast. Any readers wishing to see a catalogue should contact Colour-Rail at 5 Treacher's Close, Chesham, Bucks HP5 2HD. Check advertisements in the railway press for the catalogue price.

Below:
The 3,300hp 'Deltics' were the pride of the East Coast main line. They enabled consistent 100mph running to be introduced. Here No D9012 *Crepello* **speeds south through Welwyn Garden City on an up express in April 1962.**
Colour-Rail DE734/T. B. Owen

First published 1988

ISBN 0 7110 1767 0

Published by Ian Allan Ltd, Shepperton, Surrey; and printed by Chorley & Pickersgill Ltd, Leeds LS15 8AL

Front cover:
Leaving Southampton Central station, No 35030 *Elder-Dempster Lines* **gets to grips with the down 'Bournemouth Belle' Pullman train.**   Colour-Rail BRS308/M. Chapman

Back cover, top:
In May 1964, 'Western' C-C No D1031 *Western Rifleman* **brings a down express out of Parson's tunnel on the glorious South Devon coast.**   Colour-Rail DE169/A. E. R. Cope

Back cover, bottom:
On the Portsmouth direct line at Haslemere is a dc EMU of three 4-COR/4-BUF corridor express sets led by unit No 3120.   Colour-Rail DE844/D. Smith

CONTENTS

**A BR 'Britannia' Pacific in full flight: No 70027 *Rising Star*
climbs away from Sodbury tunnel with the up 'Red Dragon'
in September 1958.** Colour-Rail BRW672/T. B. Owen

TRACTION TRANSITION

'Steam locomotives will be a thing of the past in 10 years' time!' Thus was the author greeted when he began his apprenticeship at Eastleigh locomotive works in 1954. Yet such a statement seemed to be quite outrageous at the time. British Railways had inherited over 20,000 steam locomotives in 1948, and in 1954 new construction of steam was proceeding apace as the renewal of the fleet progressed. And, we argued, BR would certainly not be building steam engines in 1954 if they were to be scrapped in 1964. After all, steam locomotives lasted over 30 years, didn't they?

Yet, how prophetic were the words of that machinist. By 1964 there were no steam locomotives allocated to the Great Eastern lines of the Eastern Region, nor to large parts of the Southern Region. Nearly all Western Region steam had gone, and very little remained in Scotland. Only four years later, BR ended all standard gauge steam haulage.

The background to BR steam locomotive policy is detailed in my companion book *BR Steam in Colour, 1948-1968* (Ian Allan, 1986). That book highlights the several phases affecting BR's steam fleet, namely:

● The construction of further of the best Regional types
● Introduction of the 999 BR Standard steam locomotives
● Technical improvements made in the 1950s and 1960s to several classes
● The effects of the modernisation plan and the Beeching era, leading to the apparently premature end of steam traction on BR in 1968.

This new book describes the transition of British Railways to a modern, non-steam system.

The variety of steam locomotive classes taken over by British Railways was really quite incredible. Because the railways had not been nationalised until 1948, there were clearly four separate paths of steam locomotive development in this country. But the 'Big Four' railways themselves had only been formed 25 years earlier in 1923, from the amalgamation of some 123 smaller companies. Most of these pre-Grouping railways also had their own locomotive designs, and many of these survived to be absorbed into BR at Nationalisation. Thus the 20,000 steam locomotives were divided into over 400 classes — a nightmare for the operators and maintaining engineers alike.

Meanwhile, apart from suburban electrification, a few diesel shunters and the ex-GWR diesel railcars, experience on Britain's railways of diesel and electric traction was very limited. The decision to build some standard steam designs was therefore not unnatural. To bridge the gap until the standard engines were to appear in 1951, the Regions carried on building the more successful of the former railways' types. The BR Standard designs, initially planned to be built in large numbers, were supposed to enable the large variety of types to be substantially reduced. As it turned out, other factors were to prove more significant in eliminating steam on BR. Indeed, with the benefit of hindsight it might be said that the whole range of BR Standard types, with two brilliant exceptions, need never have been built.

Even in 1948, not all of British Railways was dominated by steam power. The Southern Railway in particular had bequeathed its highly developed 660V dc electrified suburban network. In the 1930s this had expanded on to the main lines to Brighton, Newhaven, Eastbourne and Portsmouth Harbour. The Brighton line featured the 'Brighton Belle' — Britain's first multiple unit Pullman train. The whole electrified area boasted regular interval timetables with no interval longer than hourly. Frequencies rapidly increased nearer to central London.

The Southern also owned a couple of unusual dc electric locomotives which it used on freight and to haul the Newhaven boat trains. A third was ready soon after Nationalisation, as were the first tentative steps into diesel traction.

On the former Great Western over 30 diesel mechanical AEC railcars had been in service for many years, including four made up into two three-car sets using standard corridor coaches as intermediate trailers. These railcars had clearly established the economic practicability of diesel traction for secondary and branch line passenger service.

Diesel locomotives for shunting duties had been successfully demonstrated on the London, Midland & Scottish Railway (LMS). The success of its 350hp English Electric 0-6-0 locomotives, which it had begun to build in large numbers, had been noted by the War Department who also took deliveries. The LMS had a few isolated suburban electric systems — third rail in London, Merseyside and Bury, and overhead on the Altrincham and Lancaster-Morecambe-Heysham routes.

The only railway to have electrified routes for freight haulage was the London & North Eastern Railway (LNER). It had absorbed the North Eastern Railway's electrified line from Newport to Shildon, which was subsequently abandoned. Its plans to electrify between York and Newcastle remained dormant. The boldest scheme, to electrify the former Great Central Railway freight artery across the Pennines via a new tunnel at Woodhead, had been delayed by the advent of World War 2 but it then went forward and was opened in 1954 by BR. The LNER also had a third rail suburban scheme serving Tyneside, part of which BR re-equipped with new stock in the early 1950s before abandoning it a few years later when fixed equipment renewals were required. More successful was the LNER scheme to electrify from Liverpool Street to Shenfield — a scheme which later spawned BR's much larger ac electrified network in Essex.

Only two railways were proceeding with designs for main line diesels at the time of nationalisation, and both were using English Electric equipment. The LMS put their 1,600hp Co-Co No 10000 on the road at the end of 1947, and thus was fully justified in screwing large stainless letters on each side claiming its LMS origin! Its mate, No 10001, appeared after nationalisation in 1948. The Southern's three 1Co-Co1s were designed under O.V.S. Bulleid's direction and appeared between 1952 and 1954. By that time diesel engine development had already advanced to enable the first two SR machines to produce 1,750hp; the last one, No 10203, was rated at 2,000hp.

Other interesting non-steam prototypes were produced soon after nationalisation as a result of initiatives by the former railways in collaboration with manufacturers. On the Western Region two gas turbine electric locomotives appeared for evaluation — one built to a Swiss design and the other by Metropolitan-Vickers. The potential for developing a large diesel mechanical locomotive was probed by the Fell 2-D-2 locomotive on the LM Region. None of these new principles was progressed further. There was also the 827hp NBL/Paxman Bo-Bo mixed traffic 'hood' unit for light, mixed traffic work, and for a time the Southern hosted a 500hp 0-6-0 diesel freight transfer locomotive.

Clearly, in the early years of British Railways the traction scene was dominated by steam in very great variety on all Regions, except that on the Southern the electrified suburban system around London was already the major passenger carrier. The table below summarises the non-steam traction inherited by BR.

BRITISH RAILWAYS NON-STEAM TRACTION: 1948-1952

Region	Type	Area of operation	Remarks
London Midland	Diesel Co-Co 1,600hp	WCML, MML, SR	Britain's first main line DMLs (2)
	Diesel Bo-Bo 827hp	Various on trial	Prototype (1)
	Diesel 2-D-2 2,000hp	Various on trial	Fell mechanical prototype (1)
	Diesel 0-6-0 350hp	Freight yards	Largest BR diesel user
	Electric (third rail)	Merseyside, London, Bury	
	Electric (overhead)	Altrincham line, Lancaster-Morecambe	
Eastern/North Eastern	Diesel 0-6-0 350hp	Freight yards	Initial batches
	Electric (third rail)	Tyneside suburban	
	Electric (overhead)	Manchester-Sheffield/Wath	Under construction
	Electric (overhead)	Grimsby-Immingham	Tramway
Western	Diesel railcars	Various secondary and branch lines	Largest user of diesel railcars
	Diesel 0-6-0 350hp	Freight yards	Initial batches
	Gas turbine 2,000/2,500hp	Main lines	Two prototypes
Southern	Electric (third rail)	London suburban	Largest electric network
	Electric Co-Co 2,000hp	Central division	Three locomotives
	Diesel 1Co-Co1 1,750 & 2,000hp	Main lines	Three locomotives
	Diesel 0-6-0 350hp	Freight yards	
	Diesel 0-6-0 500hp	Freight transfer	Prototype (1)
	Diesel trams	Ryde Pier	

BR's early policy making and direction was largely delegated by the British Transport Commission to the Railway Executive, who were thereby one stage removed from the direct thrust of current political thinking. Many lay observers were well aware of the successes being claimed for diesel traction in the United States of America. The BTC found the policy of continued like-for-like replacement of steam traction on BR was not to its taste. It could foresee the prospect of BR being perceived as an outdated industry clinging to the ideals of the past.

True, as already outlined, this early BR period did see the commissioning of the new electrification schemes which the LNER had developed, namely the trans-Pennine Manchester-Sheffield-Wath route at 1,500V dc, and the Liverpool Street to Shenfield line at the same voltage. On the Southern, large numbers of old, timber-bodied suburban EMUs were having new steel bodies fitted to their old underframes and bogies. From 1951, new SR EMUs were built to the BR Mk 1 body design and incorporated electro-pneumatic brakes (EPB) and 'lightweight' (EE507) traction motors.

Larger batches of diesel shunters were built, at Derby to the basic English Electric/LMS design, and at Ashford, Kent, to an SR/Bulleid variant. The major new development however was the diesel mechanical railcar. Surprisingly, the first group of two-car Derby Lightweight DMUs spurned the proven mechanical transmission of the successful

The fastest British Pacifics were the Gresley 'A4s'. No 60007 *Sir Nigel Gresley* stands proud in interim blue livery, posed at the opening of Rugby locomotive testing station in October 1948. Colour-Rail BRE158/J. M. Jarvis

9

Great Western cars and the numerous Irish derivatives, and instead went for a Leyland Lysholm Smith hydraulic torque-converter drive. These aluminium-bodied cars for West Yorkshire were followed rapidly by the standard mechanical cars for Cumbria, and by some from Metro-Cammell, also mechanicals, for East Anglia. These designs were clearly successful in concept, and were subsequently improved for series production.

Elimination of the Railway Executive in the early 1950s coincided with the emergence of a will to speed up the modernisation of the railways. Recognising engineers' and operators' natural (and correct) caution when confronted with the prospect of a total change of policy, the 1955 modernisation programme based the start of main line dieselisation on a series of small batches from each manufacturer, normally of 10 or 20 locomotives. The policy was to gain experience from these in regular main line service before deciding which designs to build in large numbers as standard locomotives. These classes and their early introduction are described in a later chapter.

History now records that almost as soon as the pilot locomotives were delivered there was great political pressure to eliminate the 'old-fashioned' steam locomotives from British Railways. This was to be done by buying large numbers of diesel locomotives from a range of manufacturers, without waiting for full evaluation of prototypes. Thus was born BR's family of diesel classes in a variety which has proved to be as much of a headache to maintenance engineers as it has been a source of interest to the modern railway enthusiast. The modernisation plan also produced a number of electrification schemes — most notably that of the West Coast main line from Euston to Liverpool and Manchester, but also those to the Kent coast, and to East Anglia.

Diesel development did eventually lead to further designs being more powerful, or otherwise more effective, than the modernisation plan group. Such were the two types of Co-Co from Brush and English Electric (now known as Classes 47 and 37 respectively), and the 'Hymek' and 'Western' diesel hydraulic classes.

What was unforeseen in BR's early years was the dramatic change in fleet requirement which would result from the period of rationalisation initiated by Dr Beeching during his term as Chairman of the British Railways Board. British Railways had not had the benefit of the kind of business strategic thinking which is second nature nowadays, and had gone ahead with its extensive modernisation plan without fundamentally considering what size of railway system would be appropriate for the 1950s and beyond. When the 'Beeching axe' fell, it not only caused a dramatic acceleration of the withdrawal of steam locomotives; BR actually ended up with more diesels than it needed. So occurred the premature demise of some of the less successful diesel types, in parallel with the rapid elimination of all BR's steam. Thus unfolds a fascinating story, told in some detail in the chapters of this book.

Below:
The Carlisle-Leeds main line saw heavy freight traffic thread its outstanding scenery, such as '9F' 2-10-0 No 92019 which was photographed south of Blea Moor tunnel in June 1956. Colour-Rail BRM742/A. Saint collection

Above:
The ex-LMS '8P' 4-6-2s were the most powerful BR express passenger engines. Stanier 'Coronation' Pacific No 46240 *City of Coventry* **leaves Oxenholme in 1962 with the Keswick portion of the 'Lakes Express'.**
Colour-Rail BRM259/B. Metcalf

Below:
The Southern bequeathed to BR three all-Pullman express electric multiple units, which formed the five-car 'Brighton Belle' sets. Normally two sets were used in multiple, as seen in this 1963 view near Clapham Junction.
Colour-Rail DE842/J. G. Dewing

The ultimate British 4-6-2 was No 71000 *Duke of Gloucester*, a three-cylinder prototype with Caprotti valve gear. It is seen posed at Holyhead in 1961.
Colour-Rail BRM72

The Bulleid/Raworth Co-Co dc electric locomotives used large motor-generator sets (sometimes misnamed 'boosters') to provide variable voltage control for the traction motors. The second of the trio, No 20002, is seen at Eastleigh on 10 May 1959 fresh from overhaul, painted in SR stock green with red and white lining.   Colin Boocock

Below:
At its Ashford works in Kent the Southern Region built a batch of English Electric 350hp diesel shunting locomotives of which No 15235 is seen in its original black livery. The BFB wheels specified by the SR's CM&EE, O. V. S. Bullied, are readily apparent. Colour-Rail DE167/B. J. Swain

Bottom:
Britain's first main line diesel locomotive, ex-LMS No 10000, tops Camden bank with a local service. Colour-Rail DE18/J. G. Dewing

Above:
The third and most powerful of the three SR diesel-electric locomotives, the 2,000hp No 10203, stands resplendent at Waterloo on a West of England train when new in 1954.
Colour-Rail DE629/
S. C. Townroe

Left:
The Swiss-built gas-turbine electric locomotive, A1A-A1A No 18000, heads an up express near Chippenham in 1957. Colour-Rail

Below left:
Three 1,500V dc 'EM1' Bo-Bo electric locomotives, including Nos 26022 and 26015, pause between duties at Dinting shed, in 1954.
Colour-Rail DE952/W. Oliver

The use of diesel railcars for local services was firmly established by the Great Western Railway in the 1930s. Railcar No W19W, in BR red and cream livery, was photographed at Ledbury as single line tokens were exchanged, in May 1959. *Colour-Rail DE703/R. E. Toop*

2

A JOURNEY BY STEAM

There is no better way to recall the sights, sounds and atmosphere of the steam railway than to step back in time and to undertake a long train journey in Britain in the 1950s.

In Bournemouth's Central station the announcements echo around the overall roof to herald the approach of the through train to Birkenhead. The sounds of steam are heard as a 'King Arthur' 4-6-0 clanks past and grinds to a stand behind the up starter signal bracket. We board the train, its Maunsell corridor coaches carrying a mixture of SR malachite green and BR carmine red and cream liveries. Inside, the compartments exude faded opulence — the seats have green uncut moquette covering deep cushions, and the decorative timbered walls shine under several coats of varnish. Dust flies as we brush the seats. The air inside is slightly dank — the effect of many winters of steam heating.

At the 'right away' our 'King Arthur' is opened up and soon its deep, steady bark is heard as its two large cylinders drag our heavy train up the short gradient before heading eastwards. As the train rattles through the New Forest, the view is obscured on one side as the steam from the engine beats down. Coal smuts get in through any open drop windows or sliding ventilators. Approaching Eastleigh we see on the right a very large locomotive depot with rows of steam engines on view. The eye catches a new BR standard '4' 2-6-0 next to a green 'West Country' Pacific and a dirty black 'Q' 0-6-0. The locomotive works and carriage works are only glimpsed through the stream of steam our 4-6-0 is pouring across the scene. On the long 1 in 252 gradient through the Hampshire chalk country, speed balances out at around 45mph, a good effort by our 4-6-0. Later, a short burst at 70mph downhill near Worting Junction is the last high speed running we are to experience for some time.

Another, smaller engine shed with turntable is seen as we enter Basingstoke. Leaving there we turn left on to Western Region tracks to head for Reading West. The depot at Reading is full of visually similar ex-GWR 4-6-0s and 2-6-2Ts and a brown and cream diesel railcar, all seen as we traverse the west curve, and join the Bristol main line. The rail joints clatter as we achieve 60mph along the main line before slowing for the turnout at Didcot. Here we see more Western steam power as we pass the sheds, and still more quite soon afterwards as another shed comes into view at Oxford. Here our Southern 4-6-0 is uncoupled, having boldly penetrated 'foreign' territory, and is replaced by a 'Hall' class 4-6-0 of Swindon build.

Continuing north we join the Paddington-Birmingham line at Banbury (where there is another ex-GWR motive power depot) and look out for the multitude of Western taper-boilered engines on display at Tyseley depot which passes on our left as we approach the big city. At Snow Hill station we see a 'County' class 4-6-0 decked out in dirty BR lined black arrive from Wolverhampton. A single, red-painted streamlined diesel parcels car escapes in the opposite direction. Soon after, we watch the Birkenhead train leave, typical Great Western short, sharp, loud exhaust beats hammering the ears, interspersed with the spitting sound from the engine's vacuum pump.

It is a short walk to the cavernous New Street station of the London Midland Region. One can still identify the former LNWR part from that built for the Midland Railway. A Euston train is ready to depart behind a rebuilt 'Royal Scot' 4-6-0, its LMS coaches proudly bearing BR red and cream colours. Our train to Leeds has a Stanier 'Black Five' at its head. Dark brown smoke issues forth from its chimney and lolls over the smokebox side before dispersing in the depths of the station. Perhaps that explains why we Southerners thought that the letters LMS stood for 'Lots More Smoke'!

The smoke enters our compartment as the train plunges into the tunnel under Birmingham's shopping centre. We slam the sliding windows shut, successfully trapping in that smoke already in the carriage. Back out in fresh air the windows are opened wide, and then shut again as rain drifts in!

More smoke hangs over the depot at Saltley, and — a surprise — we glimpse a former LNWR shunting tank in the shadows. Speed is steady at around 65mph on the straight towards Tamworth. A green 'Duchess' flashes by underneath with a northbound express as we cross the bridge over the West Coast main line. We pass '8F' 2-8-0s on coal trains and overtake a '4F' 0-6-0 shunting in a yard near Burton-on-Trent. Entering Derby, centre of engineering on the former LMS, many Midland 4-4-0s and 0-6-0s are seen, together with Stanier 2-6-4Ts and 2-8-0s. A 'Jubilee' 4-6-0 stands on the other side of the station at the head of an eight-coach express for London St Pancras, and (a sight for sore eyes) an ex-works 2-6-0+0-6-2T

Beyer-Garratt stands outside the locomotive depot fresh from overhaul at Crewe works.

We stand at Derby for about 7min as the engine takes water before heading on north. At Ambergate, as we prepare to leave the pleasant scenery of the lower Derwent valley, we see the main Peak line to Manchester Central curve away to the left. We suppress a desire to divert our journey to experience once more that beautifully scenic route. Through more smoky tunnels we emerge near Clay Cross and pass more coal trains headed by '8Fs', WD 'Austerities' and '4Fs'. Every yard seems to be shunted by the inevitable '3F' 'Jinty' 0-6-0T. The twisted spire at Chesterfield points vaguely upwards.

The line from Sheffield to Leeds City takes us through the Yorkshire steel and coal industrial region. Tall chimneys funnel smoke into the sky, rows and rows of back-to-back houses glint in the rain, and steam-hauled freights pass us every few minutes. 2-6-4Ts hoot as they pass on local stopping trains, as does a 'Patriot' on a southbound express. We see a Great Central 2-8-0 on a parallel route, hauling mixed freight towards Mexborough. Mining subsidence causes us to run slowly on several short stretches. The early evening sees us clanking past steam locomotive depots at Normanton and Holbeck where familiar LMS standard machines are visible, including a couple of Compounds used on the Skipton local trains and those which run across to Carnforth. The LMS part of Leeds City station is a terminus with an architecturally outstanding concourse area.

We cross to the through platforms of the station for the last train of today's journey, bound for York. Here we see a North Eastern 'D20' 4-4-0 with its large splashers, sitting in a bay with a local. A 'B16' 4-6-0 — a strange, three-cylinder, ex-NER beast with cylinders driving on its leading coupled axle — heads the York train which is formed of mixed Gresley and Thompson stock in various shades of teak and BR red and cream, with a non-corridor carriage in plain red. The old 4-6-0 shows a fine turn of speed as it accelerates out of Leeds and gives us little time to count the engines as Neville Hill shed passes on the left. We see small saddle tanks at

work in Peckfield colliery sidings, before turning north towards Church Fenton, and then the engine is opened up. The six assorted coaches ride reasonably well, if with a somewhat rolling gait, as our speed approaches 70mph.

As we slow at the approach to York we overtake a green 'A1' Pacific leaning to the curve off the Selby line at Chaloner's Whin. Our arrival at Platform 14 gives us time to cross the island quickly to see the handsome Pacific steam in, its vacuum ejector blowing loudly. How powerful this superb locomotive looks.

Next morning we join a northbound express for the run to Darlington. A streamlined 'A4' stands at the head of 13 BR Mk 1 coaches in the new maroon livery, reminding us of the former LMS colours. With a howl on its chime whistle, the 'A4's' regulator is opened, and the engine's wheels slip wildly, the Kylchap exhaust sending clouds of steam into the rafters. The train is caught on the sharp curve in the station, and will need some effort to get it moving. The hiss of the steam sanders indicates the need for a controlled start and soon we pull slowly out across the tracks leading towards the Scarborough line (from where one of the large-boilered 'K3' 2-6-0s is approaching). We see the towers of the Minster on the right, and the motive power depot on the left. The latter boasts the usual Pacific variety and a solitary 'V2' 2-6-2 outside the shed.

Our 'A4' greets the straight of the 'racetrack' with glee and its double chimney shouts to the sky as our speed edges up past 70mph. After several miles we pass the magic 80mph, clocked with ease as the wheels of our carriage rapidly mark the rail joints at their regular 60ft intervals. We manage to achieve 88mph before the vacuum brakes go on for the stop at Darlington. Why do we alight here? We want to spend a day watching the old NER 0-8-0s and 0-6-0s lugging their heavy coal trains around Teesside, to take in the sights and sounds of these old engines as they clank and grind round sharp curves with heavy 24ton hoppers in tow. Then we must return south, with fingers crossed in case we can get a ride behind the 'W1' 4-6-4 No 60700.

Exciting times!

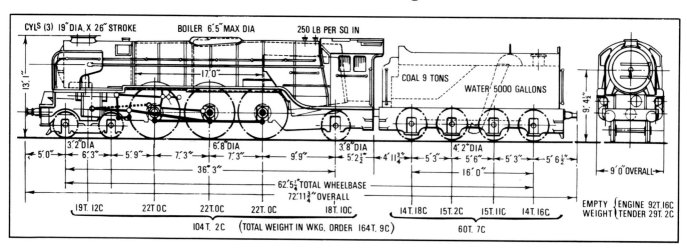

Peppercorn Class A1 Pacific. Drawing by Peter Winding

Above:
On the outskirts of Southampton, rebuilt 'Merchant Navy' Pacific No 35023 *Holland-Afrika Line* passes Millbrook with the 1.30pm from Waterloo to Bournemouth on 18 February 1961.
Colin Boocock

Left:
A giant from the 1910s, Urie 'H15' 4-6-0 No 30487 enters Eastleigh with a train of empty stock in January 1954. Colour-Rail BRS546

Below left:
'Castle' 4-6-0 No 5086 *Viscount Horne* pulls away from Reading with a Swansea train in 1954.
Colour-Rail BRW769/
F. Hornby

19

Top:
BR 'Britannia' Pacific No 70023 *Venus* thunders past Twyford in 1958 with the up 'Capitals United Express'. Colour-Rail BRW514/T. B. Owen

Above:
Birmingham New Street is host to 'Princess Royal' Pacific No 46209 *Princess Beatrice*. Colin Boocock

Top right:
Smoking heavily, ex-LMS Stanier 'Black Five' 4-6-0 No 45120 pilots rebuilt 'Royal Scot' No 46162 *Queen's Westminster Rifleman* on a 1963 express for Glasgow. Colour-Rail BRM525/A. E. R. Cope

Bottom right:
This typically Midland freight picture shows Fowler '4F' 0-6-0 No 44143 on an up freight. Note the several surviving Midland Railway semaphore signals in this 1954 view. Colour-Rail BRM836/T. B. Owen

Above:
A graceful Gresley 'A3' Pacific, No 60109 *Hermit* at Chaloner's Whin in 1957 with the 'Flying Scotsman' all decked out in the early BR carmine and cream livery.
Colour-Rail BRE472/W. Oliver

Below:
How handsome were the Peppercorn 'A1' 4-6-2s! No 60156 *Great Central* poses at Doncaster shed.
Colour-Rail BRE528/T. B. Owen

3

THE PILOT DIESELS

There was perhaps less than general excitement when the first pilot main line diesel locomotive was delivered to British Railways in 1957. No D8000 was described as a Type 1 light mixed traffic Bo-Bo, supplied by the English Electric Co (EE). Compared with the average steam locomotive, its 1,000hp was actually quite substantial for a locomotive of such relatively moderate size. At 72 tons weight and 42,000lb tractive effort it delivered an output beyond that of most medium sized steam locomotives of the period. Examples would normally be seen hauling freight trains and thus the travelling public would only see them in passing.

In appearance the English Electric Type 1 was a neat design. The lines of its cab and narrower forward section had been styled with advice from the Board's design panel. Overall Brunswick green livery was offset by a light grey roof along the length of the locomotive. Red-painted buffer beams followed traditional steam railway practice.

The eight-cylinder Vee-form engine was a direct descendant from the 16-cylinder engines of the five LMS and SR prototype main line diesels. It drove a direct current (dc) generator excited by an auxiliary generator. Traction current was taken by the four axle-suspended traction motors. The driving cab had two driving positions in opposite corners, arranged so that the driver was on the left side when facing forward. When the long nose end was leading, the view forward was restricted, but certainly little more than from the cab of a large steam locomotive. The class had no train heating equipment and was limited to a top speed of 75mph.

The first delivery of these locomotives, later to become part of Class 20, was allocated largely to British Railways' first new all-diesel depot at Devons Road in east London. They hauled cross-London freight trains, particularly on the North London line. The designation Type 1 was used by BR to cover 800hp to 1,000hp locomotives of the Bo-Bo layout. Type 2 was to cover mixed traffic locomotives of 1,000hp to 1,250hp.

D5500, which also appeared in 1957, was outwardly a much more impressive machine. Carried on two three-axle bogies, this 104-ton A1A-A1A contained a Mirrlees 12-cylinder engine of 1,250hp. It only had four traction motors, the inner wheelsets on each bogie being carrying wheels to enable the axle weight of the locomotive to be held low enough to satisfy the civil engineer's route availability requirements and yet be able to

carry the heavy, slow speed power unit. Constructed by Brush of Loughborough, 20 of these locomotives were allocated to the Eastern Region. Based on Stratford, where a purpose-designed diesel maintenance shed was built, the Brush Type 2s became popular in East Anglia where they worked, among general mixed traffic duties, Liverpool Street to Cambridge expresses.

Again, the outward appearance of this class had been styled by the design panel with good effect. Sensitive treatment of the layout of the cab windows was complemented by broad bands of off-white painted on raised strips right around the body exterior. Otherwise the base body colour was Brunswick green, with a medium grey roof, red buffer beams and black bogies and underframe details.

If memory can be relied upon, the next class to appear was the large, North British (NBL) Type 4 diesel-hydraulic. Its 2,000hp power output came from two NBL/MAN 12-cylinder high-speed diesel engines. Each engine drove through a Voith hydraulic torque converter transmission utilising three converters which were filled separately to provide more or less continuous tractive effort across the whole speed range to 90mph. The general external appearance of the full-width body and short-nosed cabs was strangely angular. Midway along the plain green bodysides were affixed nameplates commemorating famous warships of the Royal Navy. The five locomotives of this class were put to work on the Western Region's principal express passenger trains to Bristol and the West Country.

Two other Type 1 classes appeared to accompany the D8000 series, allocated initially to Stratford depot. The D8200 series were diesel-electric Bo-Bos from British Thomson-Houston (BTH) and employed a Paxman high-speed diesel engine delivering 800hp. Like the EE machines, they were single cab locomotives with a long, narrow engine compartment, but, unlike the D8000 series, they also had a short equipment compartment behind the cab. They were outwardly more stylish than the NBL/Paxman Bo-Bos of the D8400 series which used the same engine driving an AEI generator.

More types were delivered to British Railways for service evaluation in 1958. Prominent among these was English Electric's huge 1Co-Co1 Type 4, the prototype of which was No D200. This was a direct development of the Southern Region's 10203, using the same engine and principal electrical equipment but with a revised body layout incorporating a prominent nose in front of each driving cab. Like all Type 2s and Type 4s from the pilot batches, train heat was provided by a diesel oil-fired steam generator.

Five EE Type 4s were allocated to Stratford for the Great Eastern line expresses to Norwich, and five went to Finsbury Park to share the top East Coast main line work with the ex-LNER Pacific steam locomotives, a route on which the diesels' 2,000hp was to be closely compared with that of which a well handled Class 8P 4-6-2 steam locomotive was capable.

The year 1958 saw the appearance from Derby works of British Railways' first home-grown main line diesel design. No D5000, a relatively lightweight double cab Bo-Bo locomotive, carried a Sulzer six-cylinder in-line slow speed engine giving 1,160hp, supplying electric power through BTH equipment. While the body shape was neat in outline, in detail its scattered bodyside air grilles were aesthetically untidy. The employment of outside bogie frames was also an interesting feature of this design, as was the retention of spoked wheels in a modern diesel locomotive. Weighing 75 tons with a top speed of 75mph, the BR/Sulzer Type 2s were a light mixed traffic class, and began their working lives on the London Midland Region. Some of the pilot group did later find themselves on the Southern Region for a short time around 1960.

The most interesting BR diesel class to emerge in this period was Swindon's first sortie into the diesel-hydraulic arena. The Deutsche Bundesbahn in West Germany had produced its famous 2,000hp V200 B-B design in 1955. This produced its high output in a lightweight locomotive by using high-speed diesel engines and an up-to-date form of stressed skin construction which not only eliminated the use of a separate underframe (as indeed did all the other new diesel designs apart from the Type 1s) but utilised the skin on the body exterior to carry weight and traction stresses.

The BR development of this design shrunk the V200 to the BR loading gauge, but managed to retain to a large extent the bulbous, streamlined shape of the German locomotives. At 78 tons the D800 series locomotive was 55 tons lighter than the EE Type 4 and could produce the same nominal horsepower! Each locomotive had two Maybach MD650 V-12 engines delivering 1,000hp each. The engine design had the unusual feature of a 'tunnel' crankshaft in which the main bearing diameter was greater than the throw of the cranks, producing a potentially very rigid crankshaft. The Mekydro transmission used a single, permanently filled torque converter driving through a four-speed mechanical gearbox.

Three locomotives were in the pilot D800 batch. They were also named after warships, apart from the first which bore the name of General Sir Brian Robertson, the Chairman of the British Railways Board — a confident gesture if ever there was one!

By the time the 20 Metro-Vick Co-Bo Type 2s were delivered, bad news was coming from Ireland. Coras

Iompair Eireann had purchased 60 locomotives with the same 1,200hp Crossley two-stroke engine, delivered in 1955 and 1956. Within a year, Inchicore Works had collected a pile of scrap pistons and bent connecting rods. The engine design employed an ingenious system of port connections which enabled the pressure pulse of one cylinder's exhaust release to raise the charge air pressure of another. This offer of cheap pressure charging did away with the expensive and potentially troublesome exhaust driven turbo-charger used in most other designs. The Crossley Type 2s worked on the Midland main line on passenger trains, and in multiple pairs on fast fitted freight trains, including an overnight container train (the 'Condor') between London and Glasgow.

In contrast, the Type 2 Bo-Bo design produced by the Birmingham Railway Carriage & Wagon Co (BRCW) was entirely conventional, employing the same Sulzer 1,160hp eight-cylinder in-line four-stroke diesel engine as the BR/Sulzer Type 2 described previously. Electric traction equipment was by Crompton Parkinson, produced to a sturdy design with control characteristics that enabled a high starting tractive effort to be produced and sustained, thus giving these machines a sprightly performance for their size. These were neatly styled locomotives and their 70mph top speed rendered them suitable for medium weight secondary passenger and freight trains. They began their service lives by working for a short time from Finsbury Park on King's Cross outer suburban services, before transferring to Scotland where they spent the rest of their lives.

Three more designs of Type 2 general purpose locomotive were produced in small batches as part of the pilot deliveries. Two came from NBL of Glasgow and formed the only direct opportunity to compare electric and hydraulic transmissions in the same basic locomotive design. They were built with the NBL/MAN 12-cylinder engine also used in the Type 4 C-C machines. In the case of the Type 2 hydraulic B-B locomotives, a Voith LT306r transmission was fitted. The diesel-electric Bo-Bo version had GEC electrical equipment using the common layout of four nose-suspended traction motors in the bogies. In appearance the bodies were extremely snub-nosed, apparently attempting to emulate the prominent front end of the NBL Type 4 C-C but without any need for a nose in reality. Aesthetically these were probably the least satisfactory in appearance of all the pilot diesel classes. The opportunity to compare them directly with each other on the same duties was lost. The hydraulic locomotives went to the Western Region for the Devon and Cornwall areas, and the diesel electrics went initially to Stratford but soon gravitated to the Scottish Region. They could hardly have been further apart for comparative testing!

A more exciting development was the English Electric Type 2 built at the Vulcan Foundry in Lancashire. Inside a neat, medium-nosed body, supported on two bogies of similar layout to the same company's Type 1, was the least conventional of all the engines offered. Based in part on the engine design used in the prototype Deltic, which had been in service since 1955, the Type 2s had a nine-cylinder Napier Deltic engine rated at 1,000hp at 1,600rpm. Despite this, the locomotives were not exceptionally light, weighing in at over 73 tons, compared with 65 tons and 72 tons for the NBL hydraulic and electric Type 2 varieties. The 'Baby Deltics', as the EE Type 2s became known, were also allocated to Finsbury Park for King's Cross outer suburban work, and also took turns on the Cambridge buffet car trains.

Scaling 138 tons each, the British Railways-designed Type 4 diesel-electric locomotives were truly enormous machines. Laid out in similar style to the EE Type 4s, they had 1Co bogies based on Southern practice, and incorporated the Sulzer 12-cylinder engine of type 12LDA28, rated at 2,300hp. Built at Derby locomotive works, they were appropriately named after mountains and soon gained the nickname 'Peaks'. The diesel engine was interesting in two ways. Its cylinder dimensions, shared with the Sulzer Type 2s, were the largest on any BR diesel locomotive, but its 12 cylinders were not laid out in the conventional Vee-form driving one crankshaft. Instead, each bank of six was upright, and drove its own crankshaft. Set side by side, the two crankshafts were connected by gears to a central output shaft carrying the traction generator.

At 2,300hp the BR/Sulzer Type 4s were the most powerful of the pilot diesel classes. With Crompton Parkinson electrical equipment and traction motors, they had good initial acceleration and could run fast as well. Their maximum speed was 90mph, though electrically the generator began to unload above 60mph, so top end performance was not always as exciting as that of the EE4s. The locomotives worked expresses out of Euston in their early years.

Details of all these classes are summarised in the table below. All the locomotives of Types 2 and 4 had steam heat generators. They were fitted with concealed gangways for use by train crews when the locomotives were connected in multiple. Only the D800 series of diesel-hydraulics did not have this feature. Multiple working was theoretically possible by electro-pneumatic means among all the Type 2 diesel-electrics except for the pilot Brush Type 2s and the NBL diesel-electrics which had electro-magnetic through control. Headcodes were displayed by means of the folding discs introduced on the Southern's non-steam locomotives.

It was perhaps fortunate that most of the pilot classes performed adequately. The early, politically motivated decision to accelerate the building of diesel traction necessitated large numbers being built to repeat orders, without standard designs being selected. Fortunately, the Crossley and 'Baby Deltic' two-strokes were not perpetuated, and neither were the North British Type 4 diesel-hydraulics. But that is a story for a later chapter.

THE PILOT DIESEL CLASSES

Type	Builder	Number series	Rating (hp)	Engine type	Transmission	Wheel arrangement	Weight (tons)	Speed (mph)	Total built	Class (1968)
1	EE	D8000	1,000	EE	EE	Bo-Bo	72	75	20	20
1	BTH	D8200	800	Paxman	BTH	Bo-Bo	68	60	10	15
1	NBL	D8400	800	Paxman	AEI	Bo-Bo	68	60	10	16
2	BR	D5000	1,160	Sulzer	BTH	Bo-Bo	75	75	20	24
2	BRCW	D5300	1,160	Sulzer	Crompton-Parkinson	Bo-Bo	78	75	20	26
2	Brush	D5500	1,250	Mirrlees	Brush	A1A-A1A	104	80	20	30
2	Metro-Vick	D5700	1,200	Crossley	Metro-Vick	Co-Bo	97	75	20	28
2	EE	D5900	1,100	Deltic	EE	Bo-Bo	74	75	10	23
2	NBL	D6100	1,000	MAN	GEC	Bo-Bo	73	75	10	21
2	NBL	D6300	1,000	MAN	Voith	B-B	65	75	6	22
4	BR	D1	2,300	Sulzer	Crompton-Parkinson	1Co-Co1	136	90	10	44
4	EE	D200	2,000	EE	EE	1Co-Co1	133	90	10	40
4	NBL	D600	2,000	MAN	Voith	C-C	118	90	5	41
4	BR	D800	2,000	Maybach	Mekydro	B-B	78	90	3	42

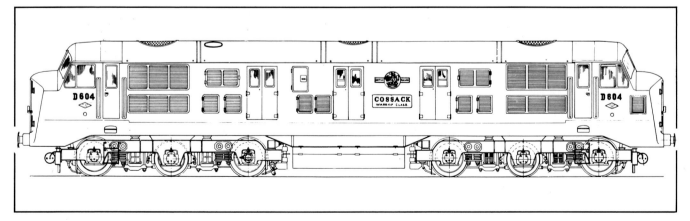

North British 'Warship' No D604 *Cossack*.   Drawing by Russell S. Carter

The first BR modernisation plan main line diesel to appear was Bo-Bo diesel electric No D8000. Its Type 1 colleague, No D8006, is seen at Willesden depot in 1962, still in original green livery. Colin Boocock

Brush Type 2 No D5507 is seen at Stratford in the early days of diesel operation on the former Great Eastern. Colin Boocock

Above:

Several of the pilot delivery of BR/Sulzer Type 2 Bo-Bos were loaned by the London Midland Region to the Eastern Division of the Southern Region until the latter's Type 3s were delivered. No D5017 stands at Ashford on 26 July 1958 with the 11.15am from Victoria which it has brought via Maidstone.
Colin Boocock

Left:

The first of the 20 Metro-Vick/Crossley Co-Bos, No D5700, passes Hest Bank with the 6.50pm Heysham-Corkickle oil train in 1964.
Colour-Rail DE505/R. Herbert

Below left:

The family likeness between the English Electric 'Baby Deltics' and their Type 4 cousins is evident from this shot of No D5908 at Finsbury Park depot in 1962. Colin Boocock

Pilot diesel-hydraulic Type 2 B-Bs Nos D6301 and D6303 head an up express in multiple at Liskeard.
Colour-Rail DE464/B. J. Swain

28

The pioneer BR-built diesel-hydraulic Type 4 No D800 was named *Sir Brian Robertson* after the Chairman of the British Transport Commission. The locomotive is seen on the WR main line at the head of a down parcels train in August 1959. Colour-Rail DE767/T. B. Owen

Below:
The first 10 BR/Sulzer Type 4 1Co-Co1s were of 2,300hp output, and for most of their lives worked freight from the East Midlands. In March 1966 No D8 *Penyghent* poses in the snow at Toton. Colour-Rail DE766/M. Burnett

Bottom:
NBL Type 1 Bo-Bo No D8401 stands at Stratford depot, already withdrawn in November 1964.
Colour-Rail DE830/M. Burnett

4

ELECTRIFICATION PROGRESS

While the main batches of diesel main line locomotives were being delivered, initial steps were being taken in three areas of the country with new electrification schemes. Mention has already been made of the Eastern Region's pioneer dc schemes over Woodhead and between Liverpool Street and Shenfield. The latter was extended to Southend Victoria in 1956. A fleet of 32 new four-car electric multiple unit (EMU) sets was built, to the same basic carriage design as the latest builds on the Southern Region. Although the earlier units used for the Shenfield electrification had sliding doors, the Southend units were considered to be of outer suburban specification and reverted to the familiar slam-door arrangement. Current collection was by overhead pantograph, the supply being at 1,500V dc. Trains ran in eight-car, or even 12-car formations in the peak periods, but four-car trains sufficed otherwise.

The Southern was proceeding apace with its electrification to the Kent coast, the first phase being from Victoria to Margate and Ramsgate. Opened in 1959, the scheme saw the first use of the BR Mk 1 main line corridor carriage design in its multiple unit form, though the SR certainly made great improvements over the standard locomotive-hauled variety in the treatment of its interior decor. General use of plastic laminates in the covering of corridor and compartment walls and ceilings was very new on BR at the time. The express sets were classified 4-CEP (corridor unit with EP brake) and 4-BEP (buffet). Less well received was the ride of these vehicles on their single-bolster bogies. These were adopted because the BR standard double-bolster bogies produced too wide a lateral swing for the SR's tighter loading gauge. Two-car units for stopping and semi-fast services were of non-corridor type, classified 2-HAP. Some of these were built new to the BR standard design; others were rebodied former SR suburban units.

Extension of the Kent coast scheme in 1962 brought the electrified third rail to the Charing Cross-Dover main line. Other routes were linked to the system so that all main lines in Kent, other than that from Tonbridge to Hastings, were electric. To improve the comfort of passengers the Phase 2 units were placed on Commonwealth bogies, but the SR's need for restricted bolster side play meant that the full potential ride improvement offered by this proven bogie design was not fully realised. The two-car sets included in the last Kent coast deliveries were odd in that each coach had a Commonwealth bogie at the inner end, and BR single-bolster bogie at the other. The SR had no Commonwealth power bogie design and anyway that bogie's equalising beam did not allow easy provision of shoegear.

A class of 25 Bo-Bo electric locomotives was provided for freight working into and out of Kent. Built at Doncaster works and delivered in 1958, No E5000 and its sisters were mixed traffic machines, capable of 90mph when used on express passenger trains such as the prestigious 'Golden Arrow' Pullman boat train. Power equipment was from English Electric, who perpetuated the motor-generator form of voltage control used originally on Bulleid's three Co-Cos. The motor half of the so-called booster unit received line voltage at 750V and drove the generator half, the output voltage from which varied in proportion to its selected speed. This enabled low voltage to be applied to the traction motors on starting, thus avoiding the traditional use of wasteful starting resistances. In effect the motor-generator set performed the same control function as did varying the speed on a diesel engine/generator unit in a diesel-electric locomotive. It also had the function of a flywheel in enabling the locomotive to cross short gaps in the conductor rail.

The bogies incorporated a quill drive to enable the traction motors to be mounted in the bogie frame, thus reducing unsprung weight on the axles. This feature was shortly afterwards repeated on ac locomotives built for the London Midland Region (LMR).

An odd feature of the Southern electric locomotives was that each had an overhead pantograph as well as bogie-mounted shoegear for current collection. The SR felt that the presence of electrified third rails in goods yards was a potential safety hazard, and overhead contact wires were put up in such locations.

For the second phase of electrification in Kent, the SR's Brighton drawing office produced an unusual locomotive design which did away with the need for overhead wires in marshalling yards. BR's first electro-diesel locomotive, No E6001, appeared in 1962 from Eastleigh carriage works. The odd feature was its ability to work on either third rail electric power or from a diesel engine. The concept was quite simple. When on the third rail the locomotive was a conventional 1,600hp resistance locomotive. But while the locomotive was in motion the driver was able to start its 600hp diesel power unit so that, when off the third rail, the diesel generator output could be fed to the traction motors. As a 600hp diesel-electric locomotive it had roughly the same starting tractive effort as when under electric power and so could handle heavy freight trains at low speeds. The power unit was based on that in the SR's diesel-electric multiple units (DEMUs).

All the Southern Region's electric locomotives delivered before 1965 were painted carriage green when new. None ever received BR Brunswick green. The introduction of the Kent coast electrics resulted in a substantial increase in passenger traffic in their area, and demonstrated the revenue benefits to be obtained from improving services in this way.

Meanwhile, aware that the French had in service the world's first major railway electrified at the standard industrial voltage of 25,000V (25kV) ac, British Railways' engineers experimented by converting the Lancaster-Morecambe-Heysham branch line to ac electric operation. The outcome was the decision to standardise on 25kV for all future schemes, except for extensions to the Southern's already established third-rail system. Advantages claimed for the high voltage ac system included the much lower costs associated with the installation of feeder and sub-station equipment, and control and supervisory systems, together with the fact that there was much greater potential for the higher locomotive power outputs required for future higher speed operation and heavier load haulage. Thus 25kV ac was chosen for the concurrent schemes on the former Great Eastern lines and on the West Coast main line. The year 1960 saw the first main line electrified with this system, from Crewe to Manchester and later to Liverpool. It was extended south to Birmingham and Euston by 1966. One hundred locomotives were built for each stage.

In this case the first 100 were clearly pilot designs, being split between five different manufacturers — most of whom supplied their own equipment. The locomotives' general layout was closely specified by BR and as a result the five classes, although different in almost all details, actually looked very much alike externally. The table at the end of this chapter lists these classes, together with all electric locomotives produced for BR during the period to 1968.

The ac locomotives were Bo-Bos of around 3,000hp which were capable of a top speed of 100mph. The majority had mercury arc rectifiers to convert the transformer ac output to direct current (dc). Mechanical tap changers selected different output voltages from the transformer windings so that the traction motors could be started on low voltage and gradually raised to 1,500V dc for full power. Their appearance bore the mark of attention from the design panel. They were painted a pleasant shade of blue (known as 'electric blue') and generally were a good advertisement for the BR of the early 1960s. Their performance revolutionised speeds on the West Coast main line.

The second 100 ac locomotives were built to a developed BR specification and construction was shared between Crewe works and EE's Vulcan Foundry. Known as AL6s (later Class 86) they were of 3,600hp, and their design benefited from the experience with the pilot types. Solid state rectification was employed — a feature which the pilot classes were later modified to accommodate. From the outset their reliability was high. They enabled timings such as 1hr 53min from Euston to Crewe to be achieved with ease and brought Manchester closer to London in time (2hr 40min) than ever before. The AL6s were painted rail blue, following the introduction of the new corporate image in 1965.

On the London, Tilbury & Southend section, ac electrification was used for the first time on a suburban line in Britain. Once again, four-car EMUs were provided, based on the BR standard carriage design but riding on Gresley type bogies. Later units had the more streamlined cab front first used on the Manchester-Bury replacement stock and later repeated on the LMR's EMUs built for main line stopping services in the northwest.

The decision to go for 25kV ac as the standard posed a problem for the Great Eastern lines. Right at the heart of their proposed network was the 1,500V dc Liverpool Street-Shenfield-Southend line, which was incompatible with the new plans. In 1960 the 1,500V route was converted to ac operation using a dual-voltage system — 6.25kV ac being used in inner London where bridge clearances were too tight for the full 25kV overhead system. The resultant spread of wires across Essex paved the way for hordes of four and three-car sets to appear, all of which were painted in BR's drab dark green which had replaced SR stock green as its standard for EMUs.

An exception was made in Scotland. For the Glasgow suburban electrification the modern, sliding-door, three-car sets were painted a shade of Caledonian blue. Striking in their external appearance, they offered a forward view to passengers in the outer carriages, enabling them to enjoy the scenery along the Clyde estuary. The first phase covered routes on the north side, between Helensburgh and Airdrie and on the Milngavie and Balloch branches. A later extension (though geographically quite separate from the north lines) covered the route out of Glasgow Central to Motherwell. Popular though these sets were, their introduction was plagued with difficulty. There were problems with transformer capacity and cooling, leading to explosions. The whole first phase was suspended after only a few weeks' operation, and reintroduced after almost a year, when the EMUs had been suitably modified. The 'blue trains' as they became known, were then the catalyst for a substantial rise in ridership.

Outer suburban EMUs for the Clacton and Northampton lines were produced in 1962 and 1966 respectively. The AM9s for Clacton were based on BR Mk 1 express stock, painted maroon, mounted on Commonwealth bogies, and designed for a top speed of 100mph. Very popular, they set new standards for a fast commuter railway, and proved to be very reliable units. For the LMR's outer suburban routes from Euston to Northampton and Rugby a more modern design using a stressed-skin body was developed. The AM10s were among the first production carriages in Britain to use B4 bogies. Their excellent ride quality caused extremely favourable comment. They remain among the most dependable units on BR. Introduced in 1966, they were painted in the new BR rail blue colour from the outset and heralded the new era of British Rail.

After a gap of some years, the Southern obtained authority to electrify to Bournemouth. This scheme incorporated a number of cost-saving features. Firstly, because traffic between Bournemouth and Weymouth did not then qualify for the cost of electrification, diesel haulage had to be used. The SR's answer was to secure through train working by using the push-pull system. From Waterloo a 12-car train would be made up of three four-car units. The front two were trailer sets with no traction motors (4-TC sets). The rear unit (4-REP) incorporated two power cars riding on Mk 6 bogies containing traction motors of the same type as those fitted on the electro-diesel locomotives. Thus 3,200hp was available to propel the train to Bournemouth where the front unit(s) were detached and hauled to Weymouth by a specially modified Type 3 diesel locomotive. The diesel later propelled its unit back to Bournemouth to attach it to the rear of the next train to Waterloo.

The other odd feature of the Bournemouth sets was that, apart from the power cars, all the stock was converted from former Mk 1 locomotive-hauled coaches and was mounted on B5 bogies. Only the 20 sets provided for stopping trains, the 4-VEPs, were wholly new.

The Bournemouth scheme was supported by the conversion of 10 of the SR's Bo-Bo electric locomotives to electro-diesels by replacing the booster unit by a Paxman 650hp diesel generator set, and adding push-pull equipment. Known as Class 74, they were joined by 43 more Class 73 variants of the original design of electro-diesel. These new ones were built at the Vulcan Foundry. The Bournemouth electrification was a landmark in the elimination of steam traction in Britain and will be described in greater detail in a later chapter.

Below:
New Wolverton-built two-car 1,200V dc third-rail electric multiple units leave Bury Bolton Street station on a service to Manchester Victoria on 1 August 1959. These sets were built to replace 1916-vintage ex-L&YR units. Colin Boocock

THE MODERNISATION PLAN ELECTRIC LOCOMOTIVES

Class	Builder	Number series	Rating (hp)	Current* collection	Electrical equipment	Wheel arrangement	Weight (tons)	Speed (mph)	Total built	Class (1968)
750V dc:										
—	BR	E5000	2,550	3R/OH	EE	Bo-Bo	77	90	24	71
—	BR/EE	E6001	1,600/600	3R	EE	Bo-Bo	73	80	49	72/73
25kV ac:										
AL1	BRCW	E3001	3,200	OH	BTH	Bo-Bo	78	100**	25	81
AL2	BP	E3046	3,320	OH	Metro-Vick	Bo-Bo	78	100	10	82
AL3	EE	E3024	2,950	OH	EE	Bo-Bo	73	100**	15	83
AL4	NBL	E3036	3,000	OH	GEC	Bo-Bo	77	100	10	84
AL5	BR	E3056	3,200	OH	AEI	Bo-Bo	79	100**	40	85
AL6	BR/EE	E3101	3,600/4,040	OH	AEI	Bo-Bo	81	100	100	86

*   3R = Third Rail, OH = Overhead
** 15 ac electric locomotives were initially geared for 80mph for freight haulage. They were all subsequently modified to standard for 100mph running.

Above:
On the other side of Manchester from the previous picture was the BR 25kV ac electrified route to Crewe. Local services were provided by ac EMUs like this one, seen at Oxford Road on a train to Alderley Edge in April 1966.
Colour-Rail DE 1085/W. Chapman

The Southern Region works at Eastleigh built the three-car EMU replacements for the former LMS units on the Euston and Broad Street dc lines. Originally in BR stock green, they were repainted dark green and lined out when overhauled, as was the case on the front unit of this six-car train from Watford seen descending Camden bank in July 1962.
*Colour-Rail DE851/
J. G. Dewing*

Centre left:
One of the pioneer ac electrics, No E3006, approaches Crewe from the north in 1962.   Colin Boocock

Left:
A total of 100 'AL6' locomotives were provided for the electrification south to Euston. They were designed for 100mph running as well as for freight haulage. No E3112 climbs Camden incline with the down 'Manchester Pullman' in April 1966.
*Colour-Rail DE708/
J. G. Dewing*

Below:
New express electric multiple units were designed to BR Mk1 stock standards to replace the Southern's Brighton express stock. The 4-CIG/4-BIG units ran on B5 trailer bogies and BR Mk1 motor bogies. Unit No 7333 passes Clapham Junction on an up service.
Colour-Rail DE338/F. Hornby

Bottom:
The first six SR Bo-Bo electro-diesel locomotives were designed at Brighton and built in the carriage works at Eastleigh. They used a 600hp 4SRKT English Electric power unit for travel over non-electrified track; otherwise they performed as 1,600hp electric locomotives. No E6001, seen standing at Hither Green in 1962, is still in SR stock green but lacks the original light grey lining band.
Colin Boocock

Above:
To test ac traction, in particular various forms of rectification of supply from ac to dc, the short line between Lancaster, Morecambe and Heysham was converted from 1,500V dc to 6.25kV ac and the former LNWR three-car sets fitted with experimental equipment. Colin Boocock

Right:
On the Great Eastern electrified lines, the ac suburban sets were repainted in unlined dark green on overhaul. In May 1960, converted Shenfield set No 081 passes Southend unit No 406 which was stabled in the sidings at Clacton.
Colour-Rail DE647/
J. R. Besley

Below right:
Alone among all BR electric multiple units, the Clacton express sets were painted in standard lined maroon livery. Unit No 623 was photographed near Shenfield in April 1963 on an up Clacton service.
Colour-Rail DE346/
R. Shepperson

5

DIESEL MULTIPLE ~ UNITS

Amid the terraced houses and mills of blackened millstone grit in West Yorkshire was a network of railways populated by former LMS, North Eastern Railway and Great Northern Railway tank engines hauling short suburban and inter-urban trains of dusty, maroon, non-corridor compartment coaches. These provided the local services on the intricate web of railway lines around Leeds and Bradford. Because these two cities are in the neighbourhood of the Pennine hills, train travel in the early 1950s was slow, as the low power-to-weight ratio of the typical steam train exerted its feeble influence. (A 2-6-2T and three carriages produced, typically, 2-3hp/ton.)

This was the locality chosen by British Railways in which to operate its first production diesel railcars. Quite clearly, considerable intelligent thought had been given to their design and layout. To improve on the steam trains they were to replace, the railcars had to have a high power-to-weight ratio. This was achieved in three ways.

Firstly, each two-car set had four 125hp Leyland diesel engines giving 500hp in all. The vehicle bodies were constructed in riveted aluminium alloy to hold down their weight, so that each two-car set weighed 53 tons in all. This produced a theoretical power-to-weight ratio of 9½hp/ton! Not only that, but by using Leyland Lysholm Smith torque converter hydraulic transmissions, the greater part of that power output was available for all the lower half of the speed range, which was most useful when accelerating from frequent stops.

Following the batch of eight two-car sets for West Yorkshire came several more deliveries of Derby Lightweight sets. These were in different configurations. Two-car sets each consisting of a power car and trailer appeared in Cumbria, some four-car sets went to the northeast, and there were even a few double-cab single cars for minor branches. All these power cars had AEC 150hp diesel engines driving through the Wilson four-speed epicyclic gearboxes that became virtually standard across most (but not all) of the subsequent BR DMU builds. The engine mounting arrangements differed from that used on the Great Western cars. Instead of using heavy outrigger brackets to carry the engines vertically, the BR cars had their engines fitted horizontally, suspended by three points from brackets affixed to the underframe.

The Birmingham firm of Metro-Cammell built some Lightweight two-car sets, examples of which went to East Anglia.

The success of these early BR builds prompted the decision to expand the construction rate. A number of other firms were invited to deliver DMUs. Four of these firms chose to develop Lightweight designs, Cravens of Sheffield, Wickham of Ware, Park Royal and Gloucester Carriage & Wagon. Apart from Cravens, these firms used integral body and underframe designs to keep down the weight of the vehicles. All employed either AEC or Leyland engines of 150hp with mechanical transmission. They were predominantly placed into traffic on the London Midland and Eastern Regions.

The cost of aluminium and of integral body construction led BR to consider the possibility of using more traditional steel carriage bodies on steel underframes. Derby Works' first offering to this style in 1956 also used the longer 64ft 6in vehicle length, compared with the 57ft of the earlier deliveries. A total of 49 two-car sets were built, each set being 15 tons heavier than the earlier Lightweight designs. In consequence the performance of a two-car set with power car and driving trailer at 4.6hp per ton was noticeably inferior to that of the Lightweights. The 150hp engines were subsequently replaced by 230hp Leyland Albion engines, driving through heavier SE4 epicyclic gearboxes. This increased the power-to-weight ratio to 7.1hp/ton and brought performance on the road up to the level required. The sets spent nearly all their working lives based at Lincoln depot.

More units emerged from Metro-Cammell, to a design with heavier drawgear such that they could be classed as heavyweight cars for operating purposes. This enabled useful tail traffic such as parcels vans to be hauled. The Birmingham Railway Carriage & Wagon Company also produced steel cars to a relatively light design, used extensively in Yorkshire and on the London Midland Region.

All the foregoing DMUs were built to a body layout with two or three entrance doors to each side and an interior layout which, while having quite a high seating density, was aimed at being suitable for secondary passenger traffic.

The first BR express DMUs also appeared in 1956, being a product of Swindon drawing office and works. The Inter-City cars were steel heavyweights, based on the standard Mk 1 carriage with Pullman type gangways and buck-eye couplings. The first were for Scotland, for the Edinburgh-Glasgow service via Falkirk — a duty which required main line quality combined with the ability to reverse direction many times a day. The sets were made up as six-car sets and included intermediate half-cab and non-cab power cars in their formations. Allocated to the depot based in the former terminus station at Leith Central, they gave good service for many years. A later batch saw initial service between Cardiff and Birmingham but soon also went to Scotland for use on the Ayrshire routes.

Another early heavyweight design (the variety was beginning to expand even in 1957) was Derby works' first suburban three-car sets. These were similar in some ways to the Lincoln cars, but had doors to each seating bay for speedy access and egress at urban stations and were not fitted with gangways.

Engines of 150hp were tried in the Swindon Inter-City and Derby suburban sets. Having two power cars for each trailer, the power-to-weight ratio was adequate for performance, so the more expensive Albion engines were not needed here.

A later Swindon three-car design was the Cross-Country type, built predominantly for the Western Region. They were outwardly similar to the Inter-City sets but had normal screw couplings and suspended gangways. The Swindon cars generally rode better than most other DMU designs and for many years they were very popular with regular passengers. The last batch of these was of seven sets for the Aberdeen-Inverness line. Another delivery of very similar Cross-Country sets for the Western Region was built by the Gloucester Carriage & Wagon Company, to an outline based on the Derby DMU design.

Derby produced large numbers of four-car suburban sets for the St Pancras and Marylebone services, and thus introduced the DMU to central London. These sets, having one trailer to each power car, needed more power than the by now traditional 150hp engines could produce. Those for the St Pancras line were given Rolls-Royce eight-cylinder engines of 238hp driving through hydraulic torque converters — the 950hp per set producing a brisk acceleration from the many stops en route to Bedford. The Marylebone sets had Albion 230hp engines and SE4 gearboxes, like the Lincoln cars, and also gave excellent service.

On the Western Region the need to replace 2-6-2Ts on Paddington suburban trains gave rise to

Below:
One of the relatively short-lived Metro-Cammell Lightweight two-car DMUs, formed of cars Nos E79051 and E79267, arrives at Barton-on-Humber on a working from New Holland in July 1957. *Colour-Rail DE493/T. J. Edgington*

more three-car suburban sets being built. Across the Western Region a basic standard DMU design based on the original Derby suburban sets was developed, and built both by the Pressed Steel Company and BRCW. Some single cars were also delivered to the same style by Gloucester and Pressed Steel, plus a few driving trailers. These last were for various branch lines. They put an end to the familiar GWR auto-trains of the steam era, and also replaced the last Great Western diesel railcars.

By 1960 large numbers of standard railcars had appeared from Metro-Cammell, Cravens and BRCW. Also emerging were a number of DMUs designed for more specialist applications. The Pennine range of hills presented problems to standard DMUs, particularly for the faster inter-urban services. BRCW produced some handsome three-car sets with 180hp Rolls-Royce engines with mechanical transmission, for use out of Leeds and Bradford. Metro-Cammell also put Rolls-Royce engines under some sets for Yorkshire and the northeast. The LM bought two batches of single-engined 238hp diesel-hydraulic cars from Cravens for use on the Preston and Manchester to Blackburn and Colne routes. These were marshalled as power twins of 476hp — useful for such hilly terrain. They were prone to fires as a result of the proximity of the fuel tank to the cardan shaft (when the latter broke or became detached for any reason), and after a most serious incident they were all quickly withdrawn for scrap.

The LMR also used pairs of 150hp engined power cars to provide higher performance on hilly routes — a rather expensive solution but one which was adequate as a replacement for the Craven diesel-hydraulic cars. Other standard type sets to appear around 1960 included new and more successful Lightweight DMUs from Derby, which were used on the LM and NE Regions in large numbers as two, three or even four-car sets. A batch of similar three-car sets was sent to Scotland, but these were to a steel body design and were used between Glasgow, Largs and Ayr. Single motor parcels vans were built by Gloucester, non-gangwayed for the London Midland Region and gangwayed for the Western Region.

Most interesting among the mechanical DMUs were the six-car sets built at Swindon for the Trans-Pennine route between Hull and Liverpool via Leeds and Manchester. There were four power cars in each consist, each power car having two Albion 230hp engines and mechanical transmission. A buffet car served hot griddled dishes. With 1,840hp, these sets were very brisk performers, if somewhat expensive to run, and were very popular for many years. The last batch of DMUs for BR was the more updated group of Inter-City cars on B4 bogies built by Swindon in 1963. These contributed to the Cardiff-Birmingham-Sheffield run, and also appeared on Cardiff-Portsmouth trains.

By 1968 the least successful DMUs were already being withdrawn, a move made possible by the contraction of secondary route mileage following the Beeching initiatives. Thus the first Derby and

Metro-Cammell Lightweight units had nearly all gone by the end of the period covered by this book.

The Southern Region, meanwhile, had decided not to go for the standard DMUs on the grounds that the Region could design a diesel-electric multiple unit (DEMU) which would be standard with its current EMU designs and which would have good performance and long technical life. The Region's immediate need was for express trains to replace the steam stock on the Hastings line, whose narrow loading gauge necessitated non-standard stock in any case. The six-car sets which emerged from Eastleigh carriage works from 1957 were unlike anything previously seen. At each end of the flat-sided, gangwayed train was a power car containing, between the driving cab and the guard's van, a floor-mounted English Electric 4SRKT diesel engine generator set of 500hp. This supplied two traction motors in the motor bogie, which was at the rear end of the power car so as to spread the vehicle's heavy weight (55 tons) more evenly. Under the power unit was an identical bogie without traction motors, designed to carry the heavier weight at that end. The trailer cars were quite conventional BR/SR EMU express vehicles based on Mk 1 coaching stock practice but with narrow body width.

The Hastings sets indeed performed very well, and while they did not set any records for high speed running, they soon earned a reputation for reliabililty and consistently reasonable running costs. The building of standard width two-car suburban sets for the Hampshire area met with such a public response that intermediate trailer cars were urgently required so that each unit could be extended to three cars. To keep up to timings it was necessary to uprate the engines to 600hp. New engines were fitted at that rating, the displaced 500hp units being fitted to further new Hastings sets as they were built. The last batch of DEMUs for the SR was for the Oxted group of routes radiating from South London. These were also of slightly narrower width than standard, and had updated front ends for greater visual appeal.

Whether one can class the Blue Pullmans as DMUs is a moot point. Certainly in later years some were converted to operate in multiple, but that was not the original concept. Intended as top-market business trains for high speed and comfort, they gave many people their first experience of travel at consistent 90mph speeds, in excellent comfort, apart from doubtful riding qualities. They were built by Metro-Cammell in 1959 and put into service on the Manchester Central-St Pancras route (six-car sets) and from Bristol and Birmingham to Paddington. They were an instant success on the peak service timings, but could not be adequately utilised off-peak and so were expensive to operate. Powered by NBL/MAN 1,000hp engines (two per set) in diesel-electric format, they were relatively conventional in traction equipment, but featured air-conditioning for the first time in postwar British stock. The Blue Pullmans were, however, without doubt the most stylish of all Britain's DMUs.

BRITISH RAILWAYS DIESEL MULTIPLE UNITS

Builder	Engines	HP (each)	Transmission	Weight (tons) power cars	trailers	Brand name	Class (1968)	Total cars
Derby	Leyland	125	hydraulic	27	—	Lightweight	—	16
Metro-Cammell	AEC	150	mechanical	27	25	Lightweight	—	98
Derby	AEC	150	mechanical	27	20	Lightweight	—	252
Swindon	AEC	150	mechanical	38	34	Inter-City	126	64
Derby	Albion	230	mechanical	36	29		114	98
Derby	Leyland	150	mechanical	36	29	Suburban	116	324
Metro-Cammell	AEC	150	mechanical	32	25		101	464
Metro-Cammell	Rolls-Royce	180	mechanical	33	25		111	45
Cravens	AEC/Leyland	150	mechanical	31	23		105	303
Gloucester	AEC	150	mechanical	31	25		100	80
Park Royal	AEC	150	mechanical	33	26		103	40
Wickham	Leyland	150	mechanical	28	21		—	6
BRCW	Leyland	150	mechanical	31	24		104	302
Derby	Leyland	150	mechanical	29	22		108	329
Swindon	AEC	150	mechanical	37	31	Cross-Country	120	195
Derby	Rolls-Royce	238	hydraulic	40	29	Lea Valley	—	60
Swindon	AEC	150	mechanical	38	33	Inter-City	126	67
Gloucester	AEC	150	mechanical	38	31	Cross-Country	119	84
BRCW	Leyland	150	mechanical	36	30	Suburban	118	45
Pressed Steel	Leyland	150	mechanical	36	30	Suburban	117	126
Metro-Cammell	Leyland	150	mechanical	32	25		102	129
Derby	Rolls-Royce	238	hydraulic	40	30	Suburban	127	120
Derby	Albion	230	mechanical	38	29	Suburban	115	168
Cravens	Rolls-Royce*	238	hydraulic	30	—		—	100
BRCW	Rolls-Royce	180	mechanical	32	24		110	90
Swindon	Albion	230	mechanical	40	32	Trans-Pennine	124	52
Derby	AEC	150	mechanical	35	28		107	78
Swindon	Albion	230	mechanical	41	32	Inter-City	123	39
Gloucester	AEC	150	mechanical	35	27	Singles	122	20
Pressed Steel	AEC/Leyland	150	mechanical	37	29	Singles	121	16
Gloucester	Albion	230	mechanical	41	—	Parcels	128	10
Cravens	AEC	150	mechanical	30	—	Parcels	—	3
BR	EE 4SRKT	500*	electric	54	29/30	Hastings (S)**	201	42
BR	EE 4SRKT	500*	electric	55	30/31/35	Hastings (L)**	202/203	96
BR	EE 4SRKT	500*	electric	56	30/32	Hampshire (2)**	205	8
BR	EE 4SRKT	600*	electric	56	30/32	Hampshire (3)**	205	87
BR	EE 4SRKT	600*	electric	56	31/32	Oxted (3)**	206	57

NB: The numbers of cars shown in each fleet are believed to be the total actually built. They do not necessarily represent the total in service at any one time.

*   Single engine per power car.

** On SR DEMUs:

    (S) = short underframe sets (57ft)

    (L) = long underframe sets (65ft)

    (2) = two-car sets

    (3) = three-car sets

Classes 201-203 were built as six-car sets, some with buffet cars. In 1964 three Hastings sets were reformed into six three-car sets using spare driving trailers from suburban EMUs. These became Class 204, and were nicknamed 'Tadpoles' because of their odd body profiles.

Right:
The first suburban DMUs were Derby-designed, long-underframe three-car sets for the Western Region. This one, photographed at Snow Hill station in 1958, was bound for Great Malvern.
Colour-Rail DE856/
T. J. Edgington

Top:
Still in SR stock green, this pair of three-car Swindon-built Inter-City DMU sets is seen leaving Stranraer Harbour in July 1963 forming the 1.30pm to Glasgow.
Colour-Rail DE428/M. Mensing

Above:
The Birmingham Railway Carriage & Wagon Co (BRCW) built many three-car sets for use in the north of England on the Eastern and London Midland Regions. One of these is seen arriving at Crewe one summer Sunday in 1962.
Colin Boocock

Above right:
Park Royal railbus No 79973 arrives at Gleneagles on the last day of operation of the branch to Crieff, in July 1964.
Colour-Rail DE415/
M. Mensing

Right:
AC Cars railbus No W79978, working the 11.45am from Kemble to Cirencester, calls at Chesterton Lane Halt, in August 1963.
Colour-Rail DE416/
M. Mensing

Below:
The high-performance Trans-Pennine sets were built for the Liverpool-Manchester-Leeds-Hull run. One of these Swindon-built sets is seen departing from Manchester Victoria for Hull in April 1961.
Colour-Rail DE935/
J. Davenport

Below:
On the Crieff branch, Wickham railbus No 79967 stands at Comrie in July 1962. Colour-Rail DE533/R. Herbert

Bottom:
The Southern Region's 500hp diesel-electric 'Hampshire' units were first delivered as two-car sets. Express patronage soon led to their extension to three vehicles, and they were fitted with 600hp engines. In its original condition, two-car set No 1114 leaves Eastleigh for Southampton terminus on a working from Alton on 13 May, 1959. Colin Boocock

One of the unsuccessful Cravens/Rolls-Royce DMUs with hydraulic transmission leaves Preston for Colne in June 1966. Colour-Rail DE939/J. Davenport

Although the Derby heavyweight twin-car sets were delivered to Lincoln from 1955 in SR stock green livery, at their first C3 overhaul they were repainted into standard dark green, as seen on this set standing at Nottingham Midland station in 1960.   Colour-Rail DE937/F. Hornby

Top:
The narrow width of the six-car 'Hastings' DEMUs is evident in this view of unit No 1012 climbing Somer Hill bank in June 1957. Colour-Rail DE488/N. Sprinks

Above:
Not every DMU journey was without problems, as is seen in this view of a failed cross-country set being steam-hauled into Banbury by Stanier 'Black Five' No 44872.
Colour-Rail BRW675/D. Smith

6

DIESELS FOR ALL

No sooner had the pilot diesel deliveries begun than it became apparent that political and other pressures were pushing British Railways towards the elimination of steam traction. The objective was dieselisation in the shortest possible time, aided by government money made available for the 1955 modernisation plan. Gen Sir Brian Robertson, Chairman of the British Transport Commission, was asked how the country could afford this. His response was to state: 'The question is whether we can afford not to!'

The result was the decision to order repeats of the pilot builds from as many manufacturers as could deliver locomotives which had been seen to perform satisfactorily in their early months of operation. No repeat order was given for Metro-Vick/Crossley Type 2s because of the mechanical problems appearing in the engines worldwide. Initial difficulties with the 'Baby Deltics' led to a block on ordering these also. The heavy NBL Type 4 diesel-hydraulics were not reordered and neither were that firm's Type 1 Paxman Bo-Bos.

Nonetheless, the rush to obtain diesels *en masse* did lead to the duplication of designs for similar duties. Of the Type 4s, the English Electric 1Co-Co1 design was built with little modification from the D200 pilot batch. BR Derby works produced an uprated version of its Type 4 with a 2,500hp Sulzer engine on board, electrical equipment for the two batches coming from different manufacturers, Crompton Parkinson and Brush, each delivering their own designs. The EE Type 4s went to the West and East Coast main lines. The BR/Sulzers swamped the Midland main lines and the Newcastle-York-Birmingham-Bristol axis. The Western Region opted for the German-based D800 diesel-hydraulics, but put MAN/Voith equipment in almost half of them, thus perpetuating NBL involvement (NBL manufactured the engines and transmissions under licence in Glasgow).

The BR and BRCW Type 2 designs using Sulzer 1,160hp engines were ordered in large numbers, the BRCW ones going to Scotland, the BR-built locomotives being allocated to the London Midland Region. Later batches received uprated engines giving 1,250hp, the BRCW ones being supplied with electrical equipment from GEC. The uprated BR locomotives received their electric traction equipment from AEI. The 1,250hp BRCW locomotives went to the Scottish and North Eastern Regions, all eventually migrating to Scotland.

Brush of Loughborough received large orders for its A1A-A1A Type 2. Only 10 years later these locomotives had to have their Mirrlees engines replaced by English Electric 1,470hp 12-cylinder diesels because of serious structural fatigue. The class was initially used exclusively as the Eastern Region's mixed traffic 'maid of all work'.

NBL also built more of its Type 2s — both diesel-electrics for Scotland and diesel-hydraulics for the Western Region. The Scots later made a case to re-engine theirs with Paxman 1,350hp engines. Of the Type 1s, the Paxman/AEI locomotives were extended to a total of 40, but many more of the English Electric Bo-Bos were built.

Meanwhile the Southern, being quite resolute in its wish to have its particular needs met irrespective of standards elsewhere on BR, required something more powerful than the BR/Sulzer Type 2s it had on loan. The SR also wanted to provide electric train heat from the outset, and its locomotives were required in the longer term to haul air braked as well as vacuum braked trains. Embracing all these requirements, the first Type 3 appeared on British Railways from BRCW in 1960. This was No D6500, a Bo-Bo based on the 1,160hp Type 2 but with an eight-cylinder Sulzer engine of 1,550hp driving a Crompton Parkinson generator which had an additional section for electric train heat output. A total of 98 of these very versatile locomotives were delivered — the last 12 having a narrower body width for use on the Tonbridge-Hastings line.

The Regions responsible for the East Coast main line were also dissatisfied with the power available from the early diesel designs on BR. A Type 4, it was said, could not substantially improve on the route timings already achieved by the top link steam locomotives. They made a case for replacing 55 steam locomotives by 22 high powered Type 5 diesels which, by dint of a 100mph running speed, could encompass a much higher daily service mileage than a Pacific steam locomotive. Thus was ordered the production batch of English Electric/Napier 'Deltic' locomotives. They packed 3,300hp into 99 tons weight, and the first arrived on BR in 1961.

More Type 3s were wanted by the Eastern and North Eastern Regions who were after a heavy locomotive for moving long freight trains, a duty for which the Type 2s were unsuitable and the Type 4s too expensive. English Electric came to the rescue with D6700 and its partners — a 1,750hp Co-Co design weighing 108 tons. Delivery of the EE

Type 3s was accomplished at a price well under that of other large locomotives of the day. They had bogies of the same general design as those fitted to the Deltics, and were equipped with the 12-cylinder version of EE's standard pressure-charged, intercooled Vee-form engine.

The WR also wanted a Type 3 but followed its liking for diesel-hydraulics. In conjunction with Beyer Peacock was developed a B-B single-engined diesel-hydraulic design using a 16-cylinder Maybach engine (built by Bristol-Siddeley) with an output of 1,700hp. Drive to the road wheels was through a Mekydro converter/gearbox unit and cardan shafts. Weight was only 74 tons. The 'Hymeks', as these useful locomotives were known, proved very popular with train crews and public alike. Although small in size they were frequently to be seen powering at speed through Swindon with heavy trains of 13 coaches from Cardiff to Paddington.

Meanwhile, the Western Region had concluded that a 2,200hp B-B diesel-hydraulic was not sufficiently powerful to make the improvements in timings to Plymouth which the market was demanding. The German railway industry was now using a larger Maybach engine, type MD655, and a locomotive with two of these installed would provide the necessary power for the WR expresses. Swindon designed a larger C-C diesel-hydraulic locomotive using two of these engines rated at 1,350hp each. Thus was born the popular 'Western' class — a 2,700hp locomotive which could develop 72,000lb of tractive effort. Stylish treatment by the Board's design panel gave these machines a most attractive aspect. Interestingly, at about the same time the Deutsche Bundesbahn had put two of these engines into a version of their V200, the V220 class, which therefore produced 2,700hp on a B-B chassis. However, the extra weight which the 'Westerns' had to carry around did help when they were rostered for heavy freight on the South Wales main line.

In 1962, another new design emerged which has become, in the author's view, the most useful and versatile locomotive of any kind that has operated on a British railway. Taking advantage of the civil engineers' relaxation of axle weights which by then enabled a large Co-Co to be built without the need for additional carrying axles, a number of prototypes had been built and tested on BR by manufacturers to demonstrate the potential of a Co-Co of around 2,700hp. (These prototypes are pictured in Appendix 1.) The Brush Type 4 employed the Sulzer 12-cylinder engine in its uprated form (2,750hp). Supplying their own traction equipment, Brush built large numbers of these locomotives at their works at Loughborough, and BR also constructed batches at Crewe works.

The Brush Type 4 has shown itself to be just as much at home on heavy block freight as on 95mph express passenger trains. Not surprisingly, the class expanded very fast, to a grand total of 512. Within them are many variations of control layout. The first 20 were built with electric train heat generators. Later ones were fitted with slow-speed crawl control for use on merry-go-round coal trains. Others were boiler fitted for steam heat, while several had no train heat supply at all. Comparison of the maintenance costs of the Brush Type 4s with those of the diesel-hydraulic Type 4s subsequently led to the Board's Chief Mechanical & Electrical Engineer deciding on diesel-electric traction for all future builds.

There was also dissatisfaction on some Regions with the poor visibility from an English Electric Type 1 cab when the locomotive's engine compartment was leading. Thus it was decided to develop a new standard Type 1 design. This had a central cab, with low height engine compartments fore and aft, each containing a horizontal diesel engine of moderate power. Of Bo-Bo configuration, this would produce a general purpose locomotive which the train crews would prefer. The resultant Clayton/Paxman Bo-Bos were of 900hp and went to the Scottish and North Eastern Regions. The last batch received Crompton instead of GEC electrical equipment, and two locomotives were experimentally equipped with Rolls-Royce engines. The horizontal engines were never entirely satisfactory, and this class, far from becoming a national standard, was subject to early withdrawal. Indeed, the last deliveries to BR of Type 1 diesel-electrics were of yet more English Electric Type 1s for Scotland and the London Midland Region!

The Western Region did build one more diesel-hydraulic class. Swindon produced a large 0-6-0 using a 650hp Paxman 'Ventura' engine and Voith transmission. Generally based on the layout of the Deutsche Bundesbahn Class V60 shunting locomotive, the D9500 series were intended to replace larger steam tank engines on freight transfer work. As the number of yards between which freight could be transferred diminished, the life of these locomotives was curtailed, and they were among the shortest-lived diesels on BR. However, many have since seen almost 20 years of successful heavy industrial service under private ownership.

Very much higher power outputs were still being sought, and towards the end of the period covered by this album there emerged the wish to speed up the London-Glasgow trains north of Crewe. Speeds of up to 100mph were required, with rapid climbs of the banks to the summits at Shap and Beattock. No existing single diesel locomotive could adequately do this (though the Brush 4,000hp Co-Co *Kestrel* could have been a contender). It was decided to build a batch of a further 50 more Type 4s which could subsequently be redeployed if the electrification of the route were completed. However, the need to run at 100mph, and the concern that was being expressed at the then increasing cost of maintaining the 2,750hp Sulzer engines in the Brush Type 4s, led BR to look to English Electric to produce a more robust locomotive embodying the excellent performance of the 2,700hp DP2 prototype.

In some respects, the BRCW Type 3 Bo-Bo design for the Southern Region represented an advance on traditional thinking. The locomotives differed from other regions' diesels in that they were equipped with both vacuum and air brakes, they could deliver an electric train heat supply and they had driving positions on both sides of each cab. In early 1968 No D6552 pauses at Eastleigh as another member of the class (a 1967 push-pull conversion) passes with a down express. *Ian Foot*

When Nos D400-D449 appeared in 1967, they had been redesigned to employ the latest 'high-tech' electronically controlled voltage regulation and rheostatic braking. They were used in pairs on Scottish expresses north of Crewe, and enabled substantial accelerations to be made to timings. Considerable difficulty was experienced with their novel design features and their availability suffered. Most of this, however, comes after the timescale of this book.

THE PRODUCTION DIESEL CLASSES

Type	Builder	Number series	Rating (hp)	Engine type	Transmission	Wheel arrangement	Weight (tons)	Speed (mph)	Total built*	Class (1968)
1	EE	D8020	1,000	EE	EE	Bo-Bo	72	75	208	20
1	BTH	D8210	800	Paxman	BTH	Bo-Bo	68	60	34	15
1	Clayton/Beyer Peacock	D8500	900	Paxman (2)	GEC/Crompton	Bo-Bo	68	60	117	17
1	BR	D9500	650	Paxman	Voith	0-6-0	50	40	56	14
2	BR	D5020	1,160	Sulzer	BTH	Bo-Bo	75	75	131	24
2	BR/Beyer Peacock	D5151	1,250	Sulzer	BTH/AEI	Bo-Bo	73	90	327	25
2	BRCW	D5320	1,160	Sulzer	Crompton	Bo-Bo	78	75	27	26
2	BRCW	D5347	1,250	Sulzer	GEC	Bo-Bo	73	90	69	27
2	Brush	D5520	1,250**	Mirrlees**	Brush	A1A-A1A	104	90	243	30
2	NBL	D6110	1,100	MAN	GEC	Bo-Bo	73	75†	56†	21†
2	NBL	D6306	1,100	MAN	Voith	B-B	65	75	52	22
3	BRCW	D6500	1,550	Sulzer	Crompton	Bo-Bo	77	80	98	33
3	Beyer Peacock	D7000	1,700	Maybach	Mekydro	B-B	74	90	101	35
3	EE	D6700	1,750	EE	EE	Co-Co	107	90	308	37
4	BR	D11	2,500	Sulzer	Crompton	1Co-Co1	136	90	127	45
4	BR	D138	2,500	Sulzer	Brush	1Co-Co1	138	90	56	46
4	EE	D210	2,000	EE	EE	1Co-Co1	133	90	190	40
4	Brush/BR	D1500	2,750	Sulzer	Brush	Co-Co	109-123	95	512	47
4	BR	D803	2,300	Maybach (2)	Mekydro	B-B	78	90	35	42
4	NBL	D833	2,200	MAN (2)	Voith	B-B	79	90	33	43
4	BR	D1000	2,700	Maybach (2)	Voith	C-C	108	90	74	52
4	EE	D400	2,700	EE	EE	Co-Co	115	100	50	50
5	EE	D9000	3,300	Deltic (2)	EE	Co-Co	99	100	22	55

* These totals EXCLUDE the pilot batches listed in Table 2.

** The Mirrlees engines were replaced from about 1967 by EE 12SVT engines of 1,470hp. The rebuilt locomotives were redesignated Class 31. The pilot locomotives (see page 25) were similarly re-engined.

† In the mid-1960s, 20 locomotives were re-engined with Paxman 1,350hp 12YJXL engines. The locomotives were redesignated Class 29 and rated at 80mph maximum speed. All others were withdrawn by 1968.

Above:
In its original condition, with WR train number clips in use, Swindon-built B-B Type 4 diesel-hydraulic No D807 *Caradoc* **poses at Old Oak Common on 25 May 1960.**
Colin Boocock

A smart pair of brand-new production-build NBL Type 2 diesel-electric Bo-Bos, Nos D6112 and D6110, stand at Stratford on 30 May 1959 during their short stay on the Eastern Region. Colin Boocock

Above:
Maroon-liveried 'Western' diesel-hydraulic No D1061 *Western Envoy* leaves Harbury tunnel with an express from Birmingham Snow Hill to Paddington in July 1963. Colour-Rail DE185/A. E. R. Cope

Right:
Less successful were the Clayton/Paxman Type 1 Bo-Bo locomotives. In June 1966, short-lived No D8525 was photographed at Barassie with coal empties from Glasgow to the Ayrshire coalfield.
Colour-Rail DE276/D. Cross

Below right:
Heading towards Cinderford on the Severn & Wye joint line, Swindon-built 0-6-0 Type 1 Paxman No D9502 was photographed in April 1967.
Colour-Rail DE690/W. Potter

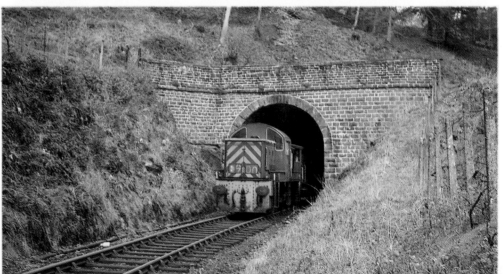

54

Above:
Over 1,100 350/400hp English Electric 0-6-0 diesel shunters were built. Most were limited to a top speed of 20mph in order to maximise tractive effort. However, on the Southern Region higher line speeds, were required and several were built for 27.5mph. One of these, No D3668, in original dark green livery, stands at Eastleigh shed, on 28 April 1959.
Colin Boocock

Below:
There was much variety in the types of small diesel-mechanical shunter ordered for BR. Here is North British/ Paxman 200hp 0-4-0 No D2912 at Rugby.
Colour-Rail DE622/B. J. Swain

Above:

The Brush Type 4s were arguably the most versatile locomotives ever supplied to a railway in Britain. Even on the Southern Region they worked oil trains one day and could be seen on Pullman workings the next. The diesel-hauled down 'Bournemouth Belle' passes through Pokesdown station near the end of its journey in 1967.
Colin Boocock

Below:

The 'Hymek' diesel-hydraulics were one of the BR design panel's most aesthetically-pleasing ventures. In April 1962 No D7012 was standing at Bristol Bath Road shed in its orignal colours. Colour-Rail DE677/H. D. Ramsey

The last mixed traffic diesel locomotives built for British Rail were the 50 Class 50s, the first of which appeared in 1967. They were allocated to the London Midland Region for use, often in pairs, on the Anglo-Scottish expresses over Shap and Beattock banks. That they also strayed on to the Glasgow & South Western route is evident from this view of Nos D435 and D429 crossing Annan Viaduct on a southbound express. *Colour-Rail DE189/D. Cross*

7

WESTERN REVOLUTION

It was the Western Region which had the honour of being the first Region to lose all its standard gauge steam power. The Great Western had always been different. The broad gauge of 7ft had put it in a class of its own in the 19th century. Then, as befitted a railway that had the courage to regauge all its main lines, from early in the 20th century the work of G. J. Churchward had given the GWR a fleet of standard steam locomotives second to none in the UK. His modern thinking had developed locomotives with free-steaming boilers, good cylinders with large (for those years) steam ports, and high tractive effort supported by good adhesion — all well able to carry out the duties allotted to them. Of particular note was his use of standardised components. Boilers, for example, fitted several different classes of engine. Cylinders were of few standard dimensions, as were driving wheels and a host of smaller parts. This enabled the works at Swindon to economise in spares and their engineers to know their locomotives in greater depth.

So proud were Great Western men of their Churchwardian heritage that his successors did little more than extend the range of locomotives, wherever possible using already established standard parts. The new 'Hall' class clearly was a 'Saint' with smaller wheels; the 'Castle' was a 'Star' with a bigger boiler; the 'King' class stretched the policy to the limit but was really little exception to it. Thus an almost complete sterilisation of design development occurred on the Great Western for, it was said, how could one improve on the excellent?

In the 1930s and 1940s the GWR was actually left well behind in the development of the steam locomotive. When BR took over the GW fleet in 1948 the best Western engines still had low temperature superheat, could only burn one, increasingly scarce type of coal effectively (Welsh steam coal) and the engines ran relatively low mileages between mechanical overhauls.

BR's answer was to replace the oldest engines with BR Standard or former LMS types, and to upgrade the more recently built express engines, the 'Kings' and 'Castles', with better exhaust systems, double chimneys and high temperature superheat. This revolutionised their performance in terms of output in everyday service, but they were still expensive in maintenance. No doubt their frequency of overhaul and the limited access they afforded for day-to-day attention to their inside valve gear were features which led to the Great Western steam locomotives being the first pre-Nationalisation group of designs to become extinct on BR.

The Western Region upheld the GW tradition of being different, however, even under dieselisation. The choice of putting all the diesel hydraulics on the one Region was doubtless dictated by the need for specialised depots equipped to deal with the exchange of major components. Certainly an opportunity was missed to obtain direct comparisons between otherwise identical diesel-electric and diesel-hydraulic locomotives. Such useful experience could have been obtained had the NBL Type 2s been allocated together, for example, instead of at opposite ends of the country. It is of course easy to comment thus with the benefit of hindsight. At the time there were other priorities.

The diesel-hydraulic fleet were all designed on similar principles to those established on the locomotives of the Deutsche Bundesbahn in Germany. The diesel engines were small in size compared with the diesel-electrics of normal British practice, and thus had to run faster to produce similar power outputs. This indicated that overhaul intervals would be more frequent, though the smaller engine size might lead to other costs being lower.

Depots were designed around the need to lift the high speed diesel engines through the roofs of locomotive bodies. The same access was necessary for changing the hydraulic transmission units. Suitable facilities already remained in several existing former GW depots, no doubt because of the frequent need to lift steam locomotives which had not benefitted, for example, from the advantages of wedge hornblocks. Thus Old Oak Common's workshop became the place to change components on that depot's new D800 'Warships', and Bristol Bath Road coped similarly with the 'Hymeks'. Newton Abbot's workshops became an adjunct to the neighbouring depot.

At most depots, echoing the situation on some other Regions, the day-to-day servicing of the diesel fleet required purpose-built sheds with deep pits and easy access to bodysides and bogies. New fuel points were necessary. These consisted universally of fuel dispensing pumps alongside tracks which were fitted with drains from which any spillage of oil was piped or pumped to a separator which enabled the waste oil to be floated off the water drainage. Waste oil was either dumped, sold, or burned in the depot heating system, depending on Regional policy. Near to the fuel point would be large tanks, never less than two in number, into which was pumped diesel oil as delivered from rail tank wagons. The need for two storage tanks arose from the necessity to let the oil in one tank settle while the other was being used for discharge into locomotives, thus ensuring that any sediment was not in suspension to be carried over to block the sensitive locomotive fuel pumps and injectors.

Because of the high mileage run by diesel locomotives between fuelling, servicing and maintenance when compared with steam locomotives, the number of depots required was substantially less. A feature of the period of transition from steam to diesel was therefore a high number of depot closures. This was accelerated when the full effects of the Beeching route cuts was felt.

The diesel-hydraulic fleet was put into main line service from 1958, starting with the C-C and B-B 'Warships'. These Type 4s took over the crack express passenger trains to the West Country and were able to time them successfully. For the South Devon banks, the steep inclines which had previously necessitated double heading of most heavy trains, the new Type 2s found use as pilots to steam locomotives. Generally the Type 4s could take all but the heaviest trains over the banks unaided. The real advantages of the B-B Type 4s at 78 tons weight was that they could pull two more coaches than, say, an English Electric Type 4 in similar

traffic circumstances, yet the 'Warships' had sufficient adhesion weight for most purposes.

The Type 2s were also used on empty stock trains and other secondary freight and passenger services. At weekends they often appeared in pairs on holiday expresses.

The 'Hymeks' were heavier general purpose machines of useful power developed from a single-engined hydraulic layout. They operated virtually all over the WR system, particularly on the Bristol and South Wales routes and on cross-country trains. They were unmercifully flogged on heavy express trains and appeared initially to respond well to such treatment.

When the bigger Type 4s, the 'Westerns', appeared, the Western Region at last had a locomotive that could permit accelerated timings on the principal passenger services. Their 2,700hp output was enough to enable level track running at 90mph and good speeds up inclines such as the long drags up from the Severn Tunnel. In common with other hydraulic designs, however, the 'Westerns' exhibited unreliability. Oddly this did not come in large measure from the engines or transmissions but from the many protective devices which had been incorporated to prevent these expensive major components being damaged by malfunction. Thus an otherwise perfectly serviceable locomotive would stop because a temperature-sensing device had stuck, or an oil pressure switch was out of adjustment. Yet the risk of damage to engines and torque convertors or gearboxes was significant, and removal of all such protection was not a course to be taken lightly. Experience did in time show what could be done with reasonable risk, and the reliability of these impressive locomotives improved significantly.

However, by this time it was becoming clear that the cost of maintaining diesel-electric locomotives was cheaper than that of hydraulic locomotives of

Below:
Modern Western Region steam power is represented by Hawksworth's 'County' class 4-6-0s. In their original condition, and painted in BR lined black, they were quite handsome machines as exemplified by No 1008 *County of Cardigan*, posing at Swindon shed in 1952.
Colour-Rail DE421/T. B. Owen

comparable size. Of particular influence was the frequency with which the higher speed engines, and the transmissions, of the hydraulics, required changing to enable repairs to be carried out. The repairs themselves were costly. Perhaps the only light relief to come from this was that there was friendly rivalry among Western depots as to which could change an engine the fastest. Laira claimed to have exchanged one engine on a Class 42 'Warship' in just under one shift, and this may well remain a record. No diesel-electric power unit in a Type 4 could be changed in anything approaching this time, seven shifts being the current established minimum.

The lower perceived cost of maintaining diesel-electrics led to two decisions which had a substantial effect on the trend of motive power developments on the Western Region. Firstly, all further new locomotives were to be diesel-electrics, and secondly, when contraction of services took place following the Beeching studies, the diesel-hydraulics were the first to go.

Thus it was that the locomotives which eliminated steam traction from the Welsh valleys coal workings were diesel-electrics. The Western received large deliveries of English Electric Type 3 Co-Cos, which took over the coal, oil and steel trains of the South Wales industrial area and have competently handled them ever since. A sizeable fleet of Brush Type 4s also came to the WR, largely working from Cardiff and Bristol.

More unusual were the locomotives transferred to the Western to enable the Region to eliminate the NBL Type 2s. Class 25 Bo-Bos were drafted in to work on the Cornish and Devon local lines, and Class 31s appeared on the Paddington empty stock trains and in the Bristol area. But these events were largely beyond the timescale of this album.

The Western was to the forefront in the acquisition of DMUs designed for specific services.

It received the first BR suburban three-car sets for the Birmingham Snow Hill and Moor Street commuter trains, and was the majority user of the two types of cross-country unit. Early Inter-City sets covered trains between Cardiff and Birmingham for a short time before being transferred to Ayrshire. The last DMUs built for BR were also on the WR, namely the B4-bogied Inter-City sets. These were also for the Cardiff-Birmingham route and later found use on the Cardiff-Bristol-Portsmouth run.

All this time the use of steam traction was slowly diminishing, first from the main lines, and later from the branches. The post-Beeching locomotive transfers enabled rapid withdrawals to take place in the early 1960s. Because the early diesel emphasis had been on the main lines it was the smaller, secondary and freight classes which lasted the longest. Even the 14XX 0-4-2Ts were still working push-pull trains in 1963. Not so by 1965, in which year the last Western Region-allocated steam locomotives ran. Thus the first Region to lose steam traction on BR was the Western.

However, regional boundary changes had recently put the Cambrian main line from Shrewsbury to Aberystwyth into the London Midland Region. Thus it was that that route became the last former GWR main line to be served by steam traction. By then Cambrian motive power largely consisted of BR Standard '4' 4-6-0s, aided by some Standard '3' 2-6-2Ts on local services. Steam on that route was displaced by Class 25 Bo-Bo diesels and a small fleet of DMUs. That final transition was lamented quietly.

Below:
GWR 2-6-2T No 4566 shunts at St Ives in March 1960.
Colour-Rail BRW473/P. W. Gray

Top:
The BR Standard '5' 4-6-0s were not welcomed by WR footplatemen who felt that their 'Halls' were quite adequate. No 73096 potters along the cliff tops above Goodrington on the Paignton-Kingswear route in May 1959. Colour-Rail BRW309/L. F. Folkard

Above:
The prototype BR Standard '4' 4-6-0 No 75000 is caught by the camera near Minffordd with a train for Pwllheli in August 1965. Colour-Rail/J. B. Snell

Above:

Pontypool Road station layout has been considerably slimmed since this photograph was taken of a 'Hall' leaving with a southbound train in 1959.
Colour-Rail BRW437/T. B. Owen

Below:

A humble depot shunting engine, Hawksworth 15XX 0-6-0PT No 1504 was pictured at work at Old Oak Common in November 1962. Colour-Rail/J. B. Snell

Above:
GWR 43XX 2-6-0 No 7304 calls at Morebath Halt on the Taunton-Barnstaple line in April 1963.
Colour-Rail BRW714/P. W. Gray

Below:
BR first painted the GWR railcars in red and cream livery, but a few later received standard DMU dark green, like No W22W seen in Kidderminster in 1959.
Colour-Rail DE487/P. W. Gray

Above left:

Gloucester-built single railcar No W55005, forming the 10.25am from Paignton to Plymouth in January 1963, overtakes 'Hall' 4-6-0 No 6973 *Bricklehampton Hall* which is waiting in Aller down loop, near Newton Abbot, for 'Warship' diesel-hydraulic No D852 *Tenacious* to bank its train. Colour-Rail DE704/ J. R. Besley

Left:

Carrying an experimental ochre livery, 'Western' C-C No D1015 *Western Champion* enters Reading with an up express. Colour-Rail DE578/B. J. Swain

Below:

Diesel-hydraulic B-B No D852 *Tenacious* approaches Teignmouth with a down express in May 1964. Colour-Rail DE376/A. E. R. Cope

The North British B-B Type 2 was not a handsome beast! No D6320 enters Hackney yard with a down freight in 1967. *Colour-Rail DE614/P. W. Gray*

8

EASTERN EVOLUTION

While the Western Region had been the first to eliminate steam locomotives from its routes, the Eastern was able to make an earlier claim. It managed to create BR's first steam-free Division, the Great Eastern.

The Great Eastern had been in need of change for many years. Its main line trains from Liverpool Street to Norwich and to Cambridge had been underpowered, having nothing bigger than the Gresley 'B17' and 'B2' 4-6-0s. The LNER also had not blessed it with many replacements for its fleet of pre-Grouping 4-4-0s, 2-4-0s and 0-6-0s. BR's approach was to attack the problems on two fronts. Firstly, the initial batch of Standard Pacifics — the 'Britannias' — were put into service on the GE expresses, which they handled brilliantly. Secondly, the decision was made to push ahead with electrification of the suburban lines. Dieselisation was also concentrated on East Anglia. English Electric Type 4s took over the top expresses and Brush Type 2s flooded the other principal services. DMUs took to the branches, and Type 1s ousted the tank engines from the cross - London freights.

In its early days, BR could boast that Stratford, in east London, was its largest depot, having over 400 steam engines allocated to it in the early 1950s. Set up as the ER's newest diesel maintenance depot, Stratford soon earned itself a good reputation. The ER had decided not to adapt steam depots but to use purpose designed depots for its new traction wherever possible. So a new facility appeared near the old steam running shed. In line with other later ER diesel depots, it featured depressed floors and high platforms in the maintenance area so that fitters and electricians could gain the fullest access to locomotives for attention. The servicing area was flat floored but was equipped with pits between the rails to facilitate brake blocking.

The East Coast main line was host to some of the early EE Type 4s which found use on such trains as the 'Flying Scotsman'. This was an interesting period on that route. Not only were early diesel locomotives being tried there, its large steam locomotives were being improved at the same time. In particular the venerable 'A3' Pacifics received new cylinders with outside steam pipes and, most importantly, double Kylchap exhaust systems. In this new form, decorated by German-style smoke deflectors, the 'A3s' took on a new lease of life and put up some of the best consistent performances of their careers. A number of the useful 'V2' 2-6-2s

were also given double chimneys and new cylinders, but that class was not completed.

The King's Cross suburban services made use of two groups of diesel traction. On the stopping services, the ancient 'N2' 0-6-2Ts with their old 'quad-art' compartment sets gave way to Craven twin DMU sets. The semi-fast services released their 'L1' 2-6-4Ts and 'B1' 4-6-0s for a variety of Type 2 diesel locomotives. These included versions from BRCW, Brush, NBL and English Electric. Only the Brush Type 2s stayed there very long. The EE Type 2s, otherwise nicknamed the 'Baby Deltics', were mostly used on the King's Cross-Cambridge buffet car trains via Royston.

In the northeast the wish to improve on the Pacifics' performance led to a preponderance of the more powerful BR/Sulzer Type 4s centred largely on Gateshead. There were also EE Type 4s in the area, though most drivers would admit to a feeling that a good Gresley Pacific could outrun one when pressed! While the Eastern Region had concentrated on the Brush Type 2s as their standard general-purpose machine, the North Eastern opted for BR/Sulzer Type 2s, and for a year or so some BRCW 1,250hp Type 2s as well.

The Eastern and North Eastern Regions were the main running ground for the English Electric Type 3 Co-Cos. They mastered the Scunthorpe steel trains and flooded the Tees and Tyne industrial areas with their dependable presence on freight. The earliest ones also joined the EE Type 4s in East Anglia on expresses and general freight.

The 49 Derby twin DMU sets based at Lincoln were to become a common sight over a wide area. They covered virtually all stopping services in the area bounded by Doncaster, Sheffield, Lincoln, Spalding, Skegness, Louth, Cleethorpes and Scunthorpe and appeared on diagrams over the Hope Valley line to Manchester. In the Leeds areas the BRCW/Rolls-Royce sets performed well on Trans-Pennine work. The true Trans-Pennine sets however were the Swindon-built six-car buffet car units which were placed in service on the Hull-Leeds-Manchester-Liverpool axis. Elsewhere in the northeast, Metro-Cammell and early BRCW sets in two, three and four-car formations did most of the local and inter-urban passenger work, added to by later builds of Derby Lightweight units.

Apart from the electrification in the Great Eastern area, interesting events took place on the Tyne electric network as well. Replacement two-car dc sets were built at Eastleigh for the South Shields

Above:
King's Cross does not look like this now! In June 1959, 'A3' Pacific No 60067 _Ladas_ is in the locomotive depot yard, an 'A1' leaves the terminus on a northbound express, while a 'Baby Deltic' hums to itself at another platform.
Colour-Rail BRE329/T. B. Owen

line. Later, when the North Tyne units and the electrical distribution equipment needed replacement, the decision was taken not to continue with electric working in the area. The whole group of services was given over to DMUs. The Gresley sets were scrapped but the later south Tyne units, being still relatively new, were transferred to the Southern Region where they became part of the 2-EPB group.

Mention must be made of the inauguration of electric traction over the Woodhead route. Until then, heavy coal and other freight trains between the Yorkshire area and the Lancashire/Cheshire industrial belt were hauled over the Pennines by former Great Central 2-8-0s. To get them up the Worsborough incline west of Wath necessitated banking. The locomotive used was BR's most powerful steam engine, the LNER Beyer-Garratt 2-8-0+0-8-2T. Upon electrification freights were

hauled over the hills by 'EM1' Bo+Bo locomotives running either singly or in pairs. Descent was to have been controlled by dynamic braking, using the traction motors as generators, but they did not prove able to hold the full weight of an unfitted freight against the down grade. The hourly Sheffield Victoria-Manchester London Road passenger expresses were initially in the charge of the seven 'EM2' Co-Cos.

An odd side-effect of the policy of giving priority to dieselising passenger and main line freight trains was the creation of pockets of steam working utilising some of the oldest locomotives in BR's fleet. At Staveley ironworks near Chesterfield, for example, a group of Midland Railway '1F' 0-6-0Ts survived their peers by being contracted to shunt the works area. However, the last pre-Grouping (1923) steam locomotives to run on BR were to be found in the industrial northeast. The coal and steel trains around the Tees-Tyne area had used ex-NER 'Q6' and 'Q7' 0-8-0s and 'J27' 0-6-0s since NER days. Their replacements were the last deliveries of EE Type 3, BR/Sulzer Type 2 and Clayton Type 1 diesel locomotives. That many of these old steam locomotives survived until 1967 is a credit to the solidity of their design.

Above left:
An 'A4' in full flight: No 60026 *Miles Beevor* leaves Hadley Wood tunnel with the 3pm from King's Cross to Leeds in February 1963. Colour-Rail BRE634/ J. F. Aylard

Left:
The WD 'Austerity' 2-8-0s were competent if unloved maids-of-all-work. No 90571 is seen on Stockton bank with a freight from Teesside to Hawthorn colliery in May 1965. Colour-Rail BRE667/ C. A. Davies

Below:
The Eastern Region placed great reliance on the ex-GER 'N7' 0-6-2Ts for its suburban services out of Liverpool Street, until they were displaced by electrification. No 69709 was photographed at Stratford shed in March 1958. Colour-Rail BRE741/ T. B. Owen

Below:
Below:
The bulk of the North Eastern 'T1' 4-8-0T is emphasised by this rear view of No 69921 at Tyne Dock in September 1960.
Colour-Rail BRE439/T. B. Owen

Bottom:
Some steam locomotives, including some ex-LNER station pilots, were restored to pre-Grouping colours in the 1960s. Newcastle Central's shunting engine, 'J72' No 68723, was one such example and is seen here in 1962.
Colour-Rail BRE22/J. G. Dewing

Top left:

The Tyneside electrified suburban network was supplied by the LNER with Gresley articulated two-car EMUs, such as this set composed of cars Nos E29316 and E29116 which were photographed at Manors station in June 1962. Colour-Rail DE1087/M. Mensing

Centre left:

'Baby Deltic' No D5908 speeds towards Hadley Wood with an up Cambridge buffet express during the Easter weekend in 1960. Colin Boocock

Below:

The LNER inherited a short line in Newcastle which had been electrified by the LNER using third rail for the route to the docks, but with overhead wires in the dock area. Nonetheless, to reach its home depot at Heaton, in 1962, No 26500 had to be steam or diesel hauled for a short distance! The two NER Bo-Bo electric locomotives were painted by BR in NER green, with splendid effect. Colin Boocock

Top:
Star locomotives, for a while, on the Manchester-Sheffield run via Woodhead were the 1,500V dc 'EM2' Co-Cos. No 27003 Diana stands at Sheffield Victoria with a Manchester train in April 1966.
Colour-Rail DE949/G. Warnes

Above:
English Electric Type 3 Co-Co No D6743 poses in the glimmer of the station lights at Sheffield Victoria.
Colour-Rail DE1034/G. Warnes

9

HIGHLAND CLEARANCES

While the title of this chapter is perhaps a little unfair, and is offered with apologies to the more sensitive of our good Scottish friends, the speed at which steam traction disappeared from vast tracts of Scotland represented a 'clearance' of sorts. Determined efforts were made to remove steam from the Highlands, from the far north lines and from parts of the Glasgow suburban area in the early 1960s.

The Scottish Region had been formed out of all the railways of the former LMS and LNER that lay within Scotland. Thus competitors became neighbours, eventually to be moulded into a single Region with its own tradition and character. It is perhaps doubtful whether inter-railway rivalries could have been so effectively suppressed without some major change like modernisation to give encouragement.

In early BR days the West Highland lines were treated as the two separate routes they had been under their former ownership. LNER 2-6-0s monopolised the trains from Glasgow Queen Street to Fort William and Mallaig, while LMS 'Black Five' 4-6-0s were the staple power on the Oban line. In those days trains for the latter destination started from Buchanan Street and ran via Stirling and Dunblane. The 'Black Fives' also monopolised the Kyle line and the route to Wick, although tank engines were the staple motive power on the branches. For a time, when the old Highland Railway 0-4-4Ts on the Dornoch branch were beyond economic repair, BR broke new ground by allocating Western Region 16XX 0-6-0PTs to this northern outpost. Stanier '3' 2-6-2Ts were adequate for the Thurso branch trains.

Dieselisation of these sinuous routes through the mountains took place rapidly between 1960 and 1962. BRCW and BR Type 2s were the only locomotives to be seen there for the then foreseeable future.

There was an interesting feature of the Scottish dieselisation which was not repeated elsewhere on BR. Early on, the Region decided to standardise on the Bo-Bo Type 2 as its standard locomotive for nearly all duties on main and branch lines that were not multiple unit workings. BRCW and BR Type 2s worked together indiscriminately on all types of duties. The 1,160hp engines tended to be used for the northern lines while their more powerful 1,250hp brethren gravitated to the West Highland and other southern routes.

For main line use the diesels usually ran in pairs.

Multiple working of Type 2s, while clearly more expensive, had one advantage over single Type 4 use. There were eight traction motors with which to attack the severe Scottish gradients instead of six. Thus a pair of BRCW Bo-Bos was quite comfortable hammering out of Inverness up to Culloden summit with a sleeping car train of 15 bogie coaches, and indeed an English Electric Type 4 would have been no match for the pair of small engines on the upgrades. A single Type 2 was equally at home on the Kyle line grinding up towards Garve summit with three coaches and a couple of Southern four-wheel vans. (Why did these old favourite CCTs and PMVs, and even the SR bogie B vans, gravitate to the north and spend so much time on these peripheral routes?)

Included in Scotland's diesel purchases were the NBL Type 2s. Experience of the MAN engines in these led to 20 of the locomotives being re-engined with Paxman units, a job completed by 1965. The remaining locomotives of the class were withdrawn in 1968.

Early dieselisation around Edinburgh standardised on Metro-Cammell three-car DMU sets for the local services. These were based at Leith depot which had been converted out of the closed Leith Central station — a policy very different to that of some of the English regions. These DMUs enabled an interval service to be operated from the Scottish capital city to Dundee, Kirkcaldy and Dunfermline, as well as along the main lines via Falkirk to Glasgow and Stirling.

Around Glasgow the thrust was to electrify the north Clyde suburban lines out from Queen Street Low Level station to Airdrie, Helensburgh, Milngavie and Balloch. The routes were wired at 25kV ac, and three-car electric multiple units designed specially. The carriage bodies were the most modern suburban EMUs on BR at the time. They had wide opening sliding doors for passenger access, and a forward view through the driver's glazed cab, ideal for a line which bordered the Clyde estuary for part of its length. Below the solebar were Gresley bogies, which did not perform well under suburban conditions, and attached to the underframe were the transformer and electrical equipment boxes.

The 'blue trains' as these Glasgow EMUs were known were launched with a strong publicity drive and attracted much increased ridership. Unfortunately, as previously described, serious problems with the transformers led to a number of explosions. The EMUs were withdrawn one weekend, and a substitute steam service hastily introduced on the Monday next. This brought out of retirement the Gresley 'V1' and 'V3' 2-6-2Ts and other assorted steam locomotives, together with rakes of old non-corridor compartment carriages which had been set aside for scrap, and these worked the electrified lines for many months during 1961. When the EMU transformer problems had been resolved by the engineers, the electric service was reopened, and traffic happily reached new heights.

The DMU services around Glasgow, for example on the Hamilton and Cathcart circles, were for a while branded the 'green trains' but without the resounding success of the EMUs. Craven and Gloucester twin sets were employed on these services. Plans were laid for the South Clyde suburban route to Motherwell to be electrified.

A localised dieselisation brought a group of seven Swindon-built cross-country three-car DMUs to Inverurie depot to work on the Aberdeen-Inverness service. Another odd event was the introduction on the Aberdeen-Ballater branch workings of a two-car battery electric unit, converted from a Derby Lightweight DMU. More important were the Inter-City DMUs which worked the Glasgow-Edinburgh expresses, and later versions of which were sent to Ayrshire.

Scottish Region's depot policy was different from that of some of the English Regions. Most were converted from former steam depots, a policy which saved cash at the time but which gave rise to the need for depot modernisations in later years. Indeed at Inverness, the diesel depot was established in the erecting shop of the former Highland Railway Loch Gorm works.

On the main Anglo-Scottish lines the larger diesel locomotives came into their own. EE and BR Type 4s arrived from England across both the East Coast and West Coast borders. Some EE Type 4s were allocated to Haymarket depot in Edinburgh for the Dundee route to Aberdeen. Nonetheless, full dieselisation of the main lines took a long time to complete. Meanwhile the sight of 'Duchess', 'Britannia' and 'Clan' Pacifics remained common on the West Coast route almost until the end of steam. On the East Coast and Waverley routes Gresley, Thompson and Peppercorn Pacifics remained in charge, but the use of the 'Deltics' on the fastest ECML expresses eventually led to an interesting redeployment of some popular steam classes.

The Scottish Region wanted to speed up the Glasgow-Aberdeen business expresses. Displaced Gresley 'A4' Pacifics were rostered on this run in the mid-1960s and enabled an accelerated service to be introduced. The trains ran over the former LMS route via Perth and Forfar.

As was the case elsewhere in the United Kingdom, dieselisation came late to the coalfields and to local freight trains, many of which were still powered by old Caledonian and North British 0-6-0s into the early 1960s. In many areas they were replaced by the Clayton Type 1 Bo-Bos with horizontal Paxman engines. Other steam replacements were made possible by the redeployment of diesel locomotives and DMUs displaced by the closure of railways under the Beeching programme. This DMU redeployment also led to the opportunity for BR to dispose of its less satisfactory types. The early Derby Lightweight DMUs were the first to be scrapped in Scotland. Later moves to replace the Clayton Type 1 Bo-Bo locomotives brought EE Type 1s north of the border.

Scotland had an active locomotive building industry which not only saw the production of the NBL types of main line diesels but also the building of many varieties of diesel shunting locomotive. Several types of NBL and Andrew Barclay 0-4-0 and 0-6-0 diesel-mechanical shunting locomotives were put to work in Scotland — most of which employed one of the two sizes of Gardner L3 engine. The English Region's preference for Drewry or Swindon 0-6-0 204hp locomotives was eschewed north of the border in favour of local products. The standard 350hp diesel-electric shunting locomotives were supplied to the larger yards in quantity. New yards had appeared at Thornton and Millerhill.

It is a sad fact that the private British locomotive builders, who had had such an enviable reputation as exporters in the past, had become so dependent on the home market in the late 1950s and 1960s that, when BR's need for massive deliveries of new power ceased, the companies found their overseas markets already in the hands of foreign suppliers. One by one the firms either ceased trading or diversified to other work. Thus the NBL factories in Springburn and Queen's Park closed, and Andrew Barclay turned to building shunters and to doing small locomotive repairs for the private sector, as well as specialised engineering work. Similar works closures took place in England.

The main BR workshops in Scotland also suffered reductions in their workloads as a result both of the gradual elimination of steam power and the contraction in the total size of the railway network. Thus Inverurie, Barassie and Cowlairs works closed, Townhill was converted to a regional wagon shop, and only the former St Rollox works of the Caledonian Railway survived the effects of the 1962 BR workshops plan. Indeed, throughout the United Kingdom the total of 32 workshops was reduced to less than 20 in a space of about five years.

With steam eliminated from all the railways in the Scottish Region by the end of 1966, future changes resulted from market requirements. For example, the need to speed up the London-Glasgow expresses led in 1968 to the multiple working of diesel locomotives in pairs north of Crewe. This interesting development is explored further in a later chapter.

Top left:
**On the East Coast main line
south of Aberdeen, 'A2'
Pacific No 60525
A. H. Peppercorn gets to
grips with the southbound
'West Coast Postal' in 1961.**
Colour-Rail SC480/
D. R. Bissett

Centre left:
**Former Great North of
Scotland Railway 4-4-0
No 62262 heads a short
freight for Aviemore along
the beautiful River Spey in
August 1954.**
Colour-Rail SC166/
E. S. Russell

Below:
**A Gresley 'A3' in its final
condition with double
chimney, improved
cylinders and German-style
smoke deflectors; No 60042
Spearmint descends
Dunblane incline with the
up 'Grampian' from
Aberdeen to Glasgow in
May 1964.**
Colour-Rail SC250/
A. E. R Cope

Above right:
A classic Caledonian Pickersgill 4-4-0, No 54471, rolls into Conon with a stopping train from Inverness to Tain in May 1957.
Colour-Rail SC126/N. Sprinks

Right:
The Scottish Region gained favour among enthusiasts by painting four pre-Grouping locomotives in their original liveries and then using them on regular trains as well as specials. One favourite was the North British 4-4-0 No 256 *Glen Douglas*, seen in 1962 at St Boswell's station during a railtour. Colin Boocock

Below:
Caledonian 0-4-4T No 55238 stands at Ballachulish terminus with the return branch train to Oban in summer 1960. Colin Boocock

Below:
Posing at Edinburgh's Haymarket shed are Pacifics Nos 60078 *Night Hawk* and 60031 *Golden Plover*.
Colour-Rail SC520/C. Banks collection

Bottom:
Type 4 1Co-Co1 No D317 is seen at Hay Fell in July 1963 with an up express from Aberdeen. Colour-Rail DE231/D. Cross

For the first 25 years of the diesel era in Scotland, the BRCW Type 2s, later Classes 26 and 27, served the winding routes to the isles. No D5337 was photographed alongside Loch Carron with a train from Inverness to Kyle of Lochalsh. *Colour-Rail DE255/D. Cross*

A BRCW Type 2 Bo-Bo of the 1,160hp variety, No D5314, heads a train of empty stock near Stonehaven on the east coast of Scotland in July 1964.
Colour-Rail DE253/M. Mensing

79

Top right:
A shunter indigenous to Scotland was the large Andrew Barclay 204hp 0-4-0 diesel-mechanical locomotive. No D2423 was photographed at Old Meldrum.
Colour-Rail DE833/ T. J. Edgington

Centre right:
The electrification of the Clydeside suburban lines revolutionised commuting into Glasgow. A pair of three-car ac electric multiple units stand at Balloch Central in 1962 before returning to Airdrie via Glasgow Queen Street Low Level. Colin Boocock

Below:
After trouble with the NBL-built MAN engines in that company's Type 2 diesel-electric fleet, the Scottish Region won authority to replace 20 of them with Paxman engines. After refurbishing, Bo-Bo No D6116, painted two-tone green, descends towards Dunblane with what is probably an Aberdeen to Glasgow express in July 1966. Colour-Rail DE245/ J. F. Aylard

10

SOUTHERN SWANSONG

If any Region could be said to have made the best of its modernisation cash, that Region must be the Southern. Its policy varied from standard BR practice in a number of important features:

● New locomotive types were kept to a minimum.
● Dual brakes and electric train heat were fitted as standard.
● New electrification was an extension of the existing dc third-rail system.
● The pace of modernisation was contained such that no premature scrapping of diesel locomotives was necessary.

The first really new arrivals were the 1951-built EMUs with electro-pneumatic brakes, which had bodies based on the standard BR Mk 1 carriage design. These were suburban sets. For many years they were delivered alongside conversions of older SR units which received new bodies to Bulleid's designs, but which were also given electro-pneumatic brakes.

In 1957 the first DEMUs were introduced on the Hastings and Hampshire lines. These were followed two years later by the new 4-CEP and 4-BEP express EMUs which had been built for phase 1 of the Kent coast electrification scheme.

The Southern Region policy was to eliminate steam traction from area to area, starting with the north Kent routes. By 1962, when phase 2 of the Kent coast electrification reached Dover, steam workings on the former South Eastern Railway were almost at an end. Its 'Schools' class 4-4-0s were moved to new duties on the Bournemouth line and on the Central Division's secondary routes to Brighton and Lewes via East Grinstead and Uckfield. Their presence on the latter enabled pre-Grouping locomotives to be withdrawn. Displaced Bulleid Pacifics, including many which had been rebuilt in the 1950s, went to the South Western Division to displace 'King Arthurs' and other favourites.

An interesting period prior to the completion of phase 2 of the Kent coast electrification scheme, saw newly delivered Type 3 diesels working on the Charing Cross-Dover line, with borrowed BR/Sulzer Type 2s providing steam heating. The Type 2s also worked local services, before they were returned to the London Midland Region.

A total of 98 Type 3s were built for the Kent scheme and initially all worked in and from the South Eastern Division. Also delivered were the 24 Bo-Bo electric locomotives of the E5000 series, and the first six Bo-Bo 1,600/600hp electro-diesels. These were for freight in the main, though the larger electric locomotives also hauled the 'Golden Arrow' and 'Night Ferry' trains.

When the Beeching cuts came they affected the Southern quite significantly away from London. The line closures in Kent, together with the downward drift nationally of freight traffic, enabled about 50 of the Type 3s to be transferred to the Central and South Western divisions. This in turn began the displacement of the modern steam locomotives. The 'Schools', some Bulleid light Pacifics, the 'Lord Nelsons' and the rest of the 'King Arthurs' met their end. The staple steam power surviving on the Central lines consisted of LMS and BR Standard 2-6-4Ts and 2-6-2Ts, and a few Bulleid 'Q1' 0-6-0s. Rebuilt 'West Country' Pacifics covered the through trains on the south coast route out of Brighton. New 'Oxted' DEMUs displaced 2-6-4Ts and SR Moguls off the non-electrified commuter services from London Bridge and Victoria.

On the South Western Division, the Bournemouth and Exeter main lines were almost totally served by Bulleid Pacifics of all classes, supported manfully by the excellent BR Standard '5' 4-6-0s. Type 3s did appear — mainly in pairs on oil trains out of Fawley and singly on some passenger trains. Many oil trains had been hauled by BR Standard '9F' 2-10-0s from other regions, and these gave way to Brush Type 4s. Indeed a batch of Type 4s numbered upwards from D1921 operated for a few years out of Eastleigh depot, only being returned home to Cardiff Canton for major examination or repairs.

Somerset & Dorset line footplatemen learned, somewhat belatedly, that the '9F' 2-10-0s were superb machines for hauling passenger trains up the 1 in 50 gradients over the Mendips. BR's desire to close that delightful railway led to no diesel traction being used on it (apart from a very few special trains). It used steam power right to the end in 1966.

A Southern Region anomaly was the Isle of Wight network. Because of its very restricted loading gauge, it had always been the recipient of old, small-profile carriages and had held on to its ancient LSWR 0-4-4Ts until they were over 80 years old. Something had to be done, and an ingenious solution was developed to electrify the Isle of Wight line from Ryde Pier Head to Shanklin at minimum cost. The third rail was laid, and second-hand low-profile London Transport tube stock was delivered to the island on the car ferry. Thus was brought about the only example in the 1960s of steam locomotives from the 1890s being displaced by electric trains.

Some of the SR's Brush Type 4s found use on Bournemouth expresses, including the 'Bournemouth Belle' Pullman train. Otherwise, steam reigned supreme on what was expected to become Britain's last steam-worked passenger main line. The proposals for electrification to Bournemouth and Weymouth had been frequently discussed, developed and amended in order to produce a sound financial case. There was to be no diesel interim solution. The installation of the third rail (or overhead if a case could be made) would see the end of SR steam.

The scheme, which has already been described, took the third rail to Bournemouth only, push-pull modified BRCW Type 3s (later Class 33/1s) working portions on to Weymouth. The continuing drop in freight volume had rendered 10 of the E5000 series electric locomotives redundant, and these were converted to electro-diesels for working Southampton boat trains and freights. The main batches of EMU stock for the Bournemouth electrification were largely rebuilt from existing BR Mk 1 locomotive-hauled coaches in an attempt to keep down costs.

The shortage of tractor units (4-REPs) at the early stages of delivery of the Bournemouth stock produced the need to run some unusual train formations. The trailer sets (4-TC and 3-TC) were put into traffic on delivery, and hauled by Type 3s.

Later, one of the push-pull Type 3s or one of the new batch of 43 Class 73 electro-diesels were used, one positioned at the rear of the train heading west from London.

By July 1967, the remaining Bulleid Pacifics, which still included a couple of unrebuilt 'West Country' examples, were being put to the test by drivers wanting a 'last fling' on express steam traction. Some of their best-ever performances were attained, including many recorded exploits of 100mph running. Sadly, on the last day general management decreed that the last 'Bournemouth Belle' should not be steam-hauled. The honour of being BR's last steam-hauled scheduled express passenger train passed to a Sunday afternoon train from Weymouth.

As it happened, the rebuilt electro-diesels were not ready in time, and neither were the last 4-REP units. The new electric timetable to Bournemouth was nonetheless started promptly, and to produce enough trains the SR used great ingenuity helped by the complete compatibility of its newly delivered stock. Thus the 12-car Bournemouth semi-fasts were sometimes to be seen with two 'small E-Ds' at the head (or rear), occasionally with two Type 3s, and sometimes with a Brush Type 4. Some workings put the electro-diesels in the middle of the train as a result of the Weymouth portion being shunted directly on to them. Sometimes a diesel or electric push-pull set would have an EMU marshalled in its formation. The author also remembers seeing a 12-car train racing towards Christchurch with a push-pull Type 3 at each end.

Right:
The Somerset & Dorset section was the Southern Region's most difficult route to work due to the climb to a summit of 811ft in the Mendips, and the many single-line sections through which summer holiday traffic had to be threaded. The southbound 'Pines Express' from Manchester Piccadilly to Bournemouth West, comes off Midford viaduct in August 1962 headed by BR Standard '4' 4-6-0 No 75023 piloting Bulleid 'West Country' Pacific No 34043 *Combe Martin*.
Colour-Rail SD141/W. Potter

Right:
The solid form of Urie 'S15' 4-6-0 No 30508 was photographed in May 1957 near the water tank and offices at Eastleigh shed.
Colour-Rail BRS570

These anomalies were largely sorted out when the last 4-REPs and electro-diesel conversions arrived. Also, in 1967 all internal SR locomotive-hauled trains were composed of air braked, electrically heated stock, most of which was of Mk 1 design. The only vacuum braked stock owned by the SR was for inter-regional services, and that was electrically heated. The only locomotives which could still provide steam for heating a train were the three Bulleid-Raworth Co-Co electric locomotives Nos 20001-3. Their only use of this facility was to haul occasional royal trains.

The end of steam on the Southern had been stage-managed with subtlety. When the final curtain had been drawn, all the steam locomotives remaining in steam on the last Sunday were gathered together at the dead of that night and hauled to the Regional 'border depots' at Weymouth and Salisbury, so as not to spoil the view for the vast majority of passengers on the Monday morning that opened up the electric era.

Above:
Unrebuilt 'Battle of Britain' Pacific No 34066 *Spitfire* climbs the 1 in 75 of Honiton Bank with a Waterloo-Exeter express in April 1966.   Colour-Rail BRS182/A. E. R. Cope

Below:
The Ventnor terminus on the Isle of Wight system was in a man-made cutting let into St Boniface Down. Adams 'O2' 0-4-4T No W24 *Colbourne* prepares to leave with a train for Shanklin and Ryde in 1961.   Colin Boocock

Below:
R. E. L. Maunsell produced the three-cylinder 'Z' 0-8-0Ts, competent engines which performed their tasks in marshalling yards with quietness. No 30953 was pictured ex-works at Eastleigh. Colour-Rail BRS429/B. J. Swain

Bottom:
At the opposite end of the scale were the diminutive 'C14' 0-4-0Ts which were rebuilds of 2-2-0T rail-motor engines. One, No 77s, was in departmental stock for use at Redbridge sleeper works, and was photographed at Eastleigh shed in 1958. Colour-Rail BRS540

Above:
The former USA 0-6-0T shunters at Southampton Docks were replaced by Ruston/Paxman 0-6-0 diesel-electric locomotives from 1962. No D2987 was photographed in August 1965 in its original livery of SR stock green, lined out in red and cream and bearing the BR crest intended for use on coaching stock.
Colour-Rail DE289/F. Hornby

Left:
The Bournemouth electrification brought new stock to the Southern Region, including the uninspiring 4-VEP units which formed the stopping services; No 7705 is seen rounding Woodfidley curve in the New Forest in August 1967. Colin Boocock

Below left:
Surprisingly, the first Southern Region trains to carry the new BR blue livery were those formed from ex-Piccadilly Line tube stock which were purchased for use on the electrified line from Ryde to Shanklin on the Isle of Wight.
Colin Boocock

**The last 'Bournemouth Belle' Pullman train approaches
St Denys, north of Southampton, in July 1967. The
locomotive is Brush Type 4 No D1924.** Colin Boocock

MODERNISING
THE MIDLAND

The London Midland Region was the first to receive new motive power under the BR 1955 modernisation plan on its receipt of Bo-Bo No D8000. It was also the last to rid itself of steam traction. Some will say these events were inevitable, being a product in the first place of the greater strength of the railways' largest region, and secondly of the fact that being the largest region rendered it more difficult to manage modernisation in the timescales of the smaller regions. Certainly, it appeared to the interested observer that diesel traction tended to infiltrate the LMR rather than be concentrated so as to achieve steam's exclusion from particular areas in succession.

The LMR did start in a positive way. Its first Type 1 deliveries were allocated to a brand-new diesel maintenance depot built at Devons Road, near Bow, from where locomotives could haul freights across London using the North London line. Otherwise, the Region's diesel fleet was in part maintained in converted steam sheds. Thus it was that the first LMR English Electric Type 4s for use on the West Coast main line shared the facilities of Camden depot with their steam counterparts. In later years, some new depot buildings did appear for diesels at such places as Cricklewood, Carlisle Kingmoor and Toton.

The use of the Type 4s on the West Coast main line was seen as an interim measure for use until electrification of the route was complete. The new diesels took their turns among the Stanier Pacifics from 1958 until the overhead wires eventually penetrated Euston station in 1966. The use of 25kV ac traction on main lines was new to BR. New depots were built to maintain the new electric locomotives at Crewe and Willesden. The new Bo-Bo fleet also received attention at Allerton in Liverpool, and at the new multiple unit depot at Longsight in Manchester, as well as at Kingmoor.

The 200 ac electric locomotives opened a new era to the British traveller. For the first time express passenger trains were run at speeds of 100mph on level track day in, day out. It was a new experience, and traffic expanded dramatically in those first years. (It is true that the east coast had 100mph 'Deltics' on the premium trains, but such speeds were not universal on all ECML expresses in 1966.)

On the Midland main line out of St Pancras, the policy was to concentrate the BR/Sulzer Type 4s on all main line trains. A comprehensive, regular interval timetable was drawn up which had an interconnecting pattern of trains heading to Sheffield hourly, alternatively via Nottingham and Derby, with a semi-fast feeding into each at Leicester. Running speeds of 90mph were reliably achieved using these locomotives. They were also quite at home on freight work, though there was a preference for using Type 2s in pairs on the heavy Toton-Brent coal workings. The power of these Sulzer Type 4s was suitable also for the steeply-graded routes of the former Midland Railway in the north. The direct line from Derby to Manchester via Matlock, the route from Leeds to Carlisle over Ais Gill summit, and the former Glasgow & South Western lines with which the Midland was always associated all needed locomotives of higher power capable of hard uphill running. The locomotives were based largely at the depots at Cricklewood, Toton and Holbeck. They also quite naturally found themselves on the northeast/southwest route from Leeds or York to Birmingham and Bristol — duties which they shared with their Brush-equipped brethren from the North Eastern and Western Regions.

Some unusual steam workings appeared about this time. Regional boundary changes put Leeds into the North Eastern Region which was responsible then for providing power for some of the Leeds-Carlisle trains. Gresley 'A3' Pacifics were thus given a chance to show their paces over the 'long drag', sharing these duties with LMR-based 'Britannias', 'Royal Scots' and the occasional 'Jubilee'. Similarly, Carlisle Kingmoor was for some years under Scottish Region ownership. That Region having already blurred the distinction between things ex-LMS and ex-LNER sometimes rostered 'A1' Pacifics on trains over Shap to Preston.

The use of DMUs had actually given the LMR its first chance of displacing steam traction in 1955. For years the routes around the Lake District had been the haunt of Ivatt '2' 2-6-0s. The Derby Lightweight two-car sets which replaced them were ideal for such scenic surroundings, giving a wide view for passengers through large windows. Most LMR DMU services were adequately handled by standard units supplied by various builders. Only in the London area did the need appear for a unit designed specifically for local duties.

The four-car sets built at Derby for the Marylebone and St Pancras suburban services may have looked externally practically identical. In fact their engines and transmissions were quite different as were their driving methods. The St Pancras cars had Rolls-Royce 238hp engines driving through hydraulic transmissions. Those for the former GC lines were given Leyland Albion 230hp engines driving through more conventional epicyclic gearboxes. Clearly, the former could show a clean pair of heels on sections where stopping distances were short, but the mechanical cars would win on fuel efficiency.

So steam traction was being ousted steadily across BR's largest region. It had second place on the WCML north of Crewe, had virtually gone from the electrified lines and had been pushed out by DMUs across the industrial regions of the Midlands and the North.

As happened on other regions, the pressure to improve the public image of passenger services meant that replacement of steam traction on the humble freights was left to last. Thus the LMR purchased large numbers of BR/Sulzer Type 2s and English Electric Type 1s (having witnessed the unsatisfactory performance of the new Clayton Type 1s) which were delivered at about the same time that the major Beeching-inspired route closures came into effect. The opportunity was then taken to rid the railway of the least successful locomotives and DMUs. The Metro-Vick/Crossley Co-Bos were scrapped, as were many early Derby Lightweight DMUs. Type 2s were displaced to the Western Region.

Despite the successful introduction of the Brush Type 4s in large numbers, particularly on the new Freightliner container services and merry-go-round coal trains, early experience with the class was fraught with engine problems. There was a perceived need for more Type 4 power on the LMR because of the wish to speed up trains on the Crewe-Carlisle-Glasgow section. There was also at that time (the later 1960s) a squeeze on capital for such projects, as the railways were operating under much stronger financial control than had been evident in the pre-Beeching years. A novel solution to the dilemma was to lease from the English Electric Company a fleet of 50 2,700hp locomotives.

Nos D400-49 were Co-Cos based on the DP2 prototype (see page 103). Actually, their nearest counterpart was the batch of 10 Co-Cos delivered to Portugal just previously, to which they were visually not dissimilar. BR's design team required the locomotives to be fitted with rheostatic braking and the use of electronics in their load regulation was specified. The same 16-cylinder engine that had been used in No 10000 and the EE Type 4s was provided, but this was uprated to 2,700hp with higher turbo-charger pressures and intercooling. The bogies and traction motors were basically the same as used on the 3,300hp 'Deltics' and the EE Type 3s.

To improve timings on the Anglo-Scottish expresses, these locomotives (known as Class 50s in the 1968 reclassification scheme) were run in multiple pairs from Crewe to Glasgow, producing a very potent traction form for the hills of that route. Their introduction enabled the further redeployment of older diesels, and precipitated the final end of steam locomotive haulage on the standard gauge rails of BR.

The last few months of steam on British Railways saw dwindling activity centred on the Buxton stone trains and on general secondary services in the Manchester and Preston areas. Stanier 'Black Five' 4-6-0s and '8F' 2-8-0s held the fort among BR Standard '4' and '5' 4-6-0s and WD 'Austerity' 2-8-0s. A solitary 'Britannia' became BR's last operational Pacific.

High fares were charged for the special trains on the last day. 'Britannia' Pacific No 70013 *Oliver Cromwell* and a pair of 'Black Fives' performed well on their nostalgic and historic final runs. A few tears were shed and 165 years of steam traction on the railways of Britain came to an end — or so we all thought at the time. Some small steam tank locomotives survived in industrial use until around 1980, and by then of course the steam preservation movement was in full swing. But in 1968, British Rail was looking forward to its cleaner, faster and brighter future without steam locomotives to blot either its modern image or the skyline.

Top right:

Rebuilt 'Patriot' 4-6-0 No 45521 *Rhyl* passes the pick-up point for the travelling Post Office near Lancaster in June 1963 while making heavy weather with a main line fitted freight. Colour-Rail BRM168/A. E. R. Cope

Bottom right:

How nice the Lune Gorge looked without the M6 motorway! Stanier 2-6-4T No 42593 pilots 'Jubilee' 4-6-0 No 45698 *Mars* with a Liverpool to Glasgow train in June 1961. Colour-Rail BRM311/D. Cross

The London Midland Region's supreme express passenger train was the 'Caledonian' from London to Glasgow. It is seen here leaving the old Euston station in March 1960 with Stanier 'Coronation' Pacific No 46255 *City of Hereford* at its head.   Colour-Rail BRM404/J. P. Mullett

St Pancras as it used to be. Two 'Jubilee' 4-6-0s confront the gasholders at the north end of the station in October 1956. No 45639 *Raleigh* leaves with the 2.15pm to Bradford while No 45622 *Nyasaland* waits in the background.
Colour-Rail BRM287/T. J. Edgington

Above:
A remnant of the Lancashire & Yorkshire Railway, Aspinall 0-6-0ST No 51381 rests outside Sowerby Bridge depot in April 1955.
Colour-Rail BRM967/
T. B. Owen

Right:
On the Croxley Green branch, one of the last of the former LMS three-car EMUs calls at Watford West in 1962.
Colour-Rail/N. F. Gurley

Below right:
Carnforth is host to an historic scene in this 1967 view of Crossley Co-Bo No D5711 leaving with a Barrow to Morecambe stopping train. Condemned steam locomotives await their last journeys for scrap.
Colour-Rail DE802/
B. Magilton

Above:
A BR/Sulzer 2,500hp Type 4 1Co-Co1 calls at Grindleford in 1966 with a Manchester to Sheffield stopping train.
Colin Boocock

Below:
The 'Blue Pullman' diesel-electric set which worked the morning up 'Manchester Pullman' service used to fill in on a St Pancras-Leicester return run (later extended to Nottingham) before its evening return north. The smart formation is seen at Leicester London Road on 5 September 1960. Colin Boocock

At Banbury Merton Street, terminus of the line from Buckingham, rests Derby 'alloy' single DMU car No M79901 in August 1956. *Colour-Rail DE858/T. J. Edgington*

TRAUMA OR TRIUMPH?

The years from 1948 to 1968 saw the shape, size, composition, traction, coaching stock and image of British Railways change completely. Indeed, even the name had changed. In 1948 it was British Railways — a vast conglomerate merged from the old companies; in 1968 BR was a slimmer, tighter, more modern whole known to all as British Rail. To the traveller the most fundamental change (except at those places where the railway had disappeared completely) was the elimination of the steam locomotives. To help us assess the changes, and to decide whether they represented trauma or triumph, let us attempt to retrace, in 1968, the 1950s journey described in Chapter 2.

In Bournemouth station the taped announcements echo around the overall roof to herald the approach of the fast train to Waterloo. The soft beat of a Westinghouse compressor is heard as the 4-REP unit glides past, its electro-pneumatic brakes hissing as it stops by the multiple-aspect colour light signal at the platform end. Two similar-looking 4-TC trailer sets propelled by a Class 33/1 (BRCW Type 3) diesel arrive from Weymouth and couple on the rear. The diesel is uncoupled. The train is in plain rail blue livery except for the rear 4-TC set which has been recently repainted in blue and grey.

At the sound of the guard's bell (two strokes) we hear the brakes released and the traction motor gears whine quietly as the London train glides out of the station. We stay on the platform and await the arrival of the through train to Manchester. A two-tone green Class 47 (Brush Type 4) with all-over yellow ends arrives hauling a train of Mk 1 coaches. The majority are painted blue and grey but one is still in maroon livery. Inside, the uncut red moquette is clean if a bit worn, and the train is warm. Steam oozes from drain valves and hoses between the carriages. Leaving Bournemouth our big diesel roars loudly as we climb quicky upgrade heading eastwards. Wild ponies are seen in the New Forest as the train slows for the 75mph restriction round Woodfidley curve. Approaching Eastleigh we glance over to where the engine sheds used to be. Now a few train sets stand awaiting entry to the combined locomotive and carriage works. The modern diesel shed is in the background, and a Sulzer Type 3 in rail blue stands adjacent to one still carrying the old dark green colour.

On the long 1 in 252 gradient through the Hampshire chalk country, our speed balances out between 75 and 80mph. Later, a burst of 90mph

before Worting Junction heralds our approach to Basingstoke. New factories and office blocks line the railway. Leaving there we turn left, heading north and joining the Western Region tracks at Southcote Junction near Reading. Approaching the main station we pass the traction maintenance depot on our left, seeing several suburban DMU sets, a 'Hymek' diesel-hydraulic and a Southern Class 33.

Another Class 47 backs on to the west end of the train, and after about 12min we are away again, heading rapidly at about 85mph along the main line on continuously welded rail before slowing for the ladder turnouts at Didcot. Here we glimpse some preserved WR steam power as we pass the former engine sheds while our train accelerates northwards, soon arriving for a brief halt at Oxford.

Continuing north we join the former Paddington-Birmingham main line at Banbury, and as we approach the big city we look out for the DMU sheds at Tyseley, alongside part of the former steam shed which now hosts a small preserved steam collection.

At New Street station we glimpse a new Class 86 electric locomotive which is about to leave with a Euston express made up of Mk 2 stock, and a maroon 'Warship' prepares to leave the other end of this modern, if gloomy, station bound for Plymouth. Plain blue suburban DMUs scurry in and out, trailing twin plumes of faint grey exhaust. Our train to Leeds has a Class 46 1Co-Co1 at the head. We leave through the long tunnels, slamming into the curves as the train accelerates out of Birmingham.

Diesels of all sizes surround the fuel point at Saltley. Our speed rises to over 80mph on the straight towards Tamworth. An electric blue Class 85 flashes by underneath with a northbound Inter-City train as we cross the bridge over the West Coast main line. We pass a slow-speed-fitted Class 47 on a merry-go-round coal train near Burton-on-Trent. Entering Derby, the centre of mechanical and electrical engineering on BR, a few Class 25s and 45s are seen together with a green DMU. A Class 45 stands on the other side of the station with a nine-coach train for London St Pancras. A freshly overhauled Class 24 stands outside the works.

We stop only briefly at Derby before heading north. At Ambergate the main line swings right as the single track of the Matlock branch curves away to the left. Through tunnels we emerge near Clay

Cross and pass another merry-go-round coal train with the inevitable Class 47 at its head. The twisted spire at Chesterfield points vaguely upwards.

The line from Sheffield to Leeds takes us through the Yorkshire steel and coal industrial region. Tall chimneys funnel smoke into the sky, and tower blocks of flats dominate the skyline. A pair of Class 20s passes with a string of bogie bolster wagons carrying steel billets. We see a Class 31 on a parallel route hauling mixed freight towards Mexborough. Mining subsidence causes us to run slowly on several short stretches. The afternoon sun sees us passing the rationalised layout at Normanton. More Class 45s are glimpsed at Holbeck diesel depot. We arrive at the modernised Leeds station.

Here we change on to a four-car Metro-Cammell DMU bound for York. We depart, leaving behind a station full of local DMUs as we accelerate past their home depot at Neville Hill. We see a small maroon saddle tank shunting at Peckfield colliery, before we turn north towards Church Fenton, and then we accelerate to our DMU's maximum permitted speed, our single-bolster bogies hunting on the welded rails.

As we slow for the approach to York we overtake a blue 'Deltic' leaning to the curve off the Selby line at Chaloner's Whin. As we alight at Platform 14 the 'Deltic' glides in at the opposite platform face, its Napier engines thrumming deeply. How powerful this classic locomotive looks. We join its train of the latest air-conditioned Mk 2d Inter-City stock for the run to Darlington.

With a hoot on its horn the 'Deltic's' power controller is opened up gently and the train glides slowly out of York. We see the towers of the Minster on our right, and the diesel depot on the left. Outside it are the usual examples of Classes 40, 31, 25, 37 and DMUs.

Our 'Deltic' greets the straight of the 'racetrack' with glee and its engines roar heavenwards as speed rapidly rises past 80mph, eases upwards into the 90s and eventually tips the magic 100mph. Inside the air-conditioned coaches the ride is smooth and quiet. The passengers have little impression of the speed we are doing, before the brakes come on for the stop at Darlington. Why do we alight here? We want to spend a day watching NCB steam tank engines shunting the yards around the coal mines, before steam disappears from the British industrial scene. And then we must return south, almost certainly to ride again in air-conditioned comfort behind a 'Deltic' at 100mph. Exciting times!

What were the main changes the railway customer saw in the 20 years between the journey described in Chapter 2 and that described here? The trains were cleaner, certainly. The Beeching cuts and route rationalisations had closed off some travel opportunities (such as the Bournemouth-Birkenhead through train). Many fewer freight trains were seen, though the merry-go-round coal services brought new efficiency to that operation.

Travel was generally smoother in 1968 than in 1948 and, except on secondary services, noticeably faster. Higher standards were evident on the top Inter-City routes, possibly in greater contrast than before to the cross-country and local services. There were fewer depots in which to service and maintain locomotives and steam locomotives had disappeared from BR.

Hindsight can be a mixed blessing. With hindsight we can question whether the BR Standard steam classes should have been built at all. We can question why the Beeching approach to deciding on the most economic system size for BR was not done *before* massive investment in diesel locomotives and DMUs, many of which were prematurely rendered surplus to requirements. In the imaginary ideal world, BR might have developed a few diesel prototypes to high reliability in the early 1950s and then ordered enough to replace the ageing steam fleet area by area. Orders might have been spread over sufficient years to discourage private locomotive suppliers from abandoning their overseas markets. A total of about five standard diesel classes might have been built, to meet all requirements. Capital expenditure could have been much less.

But the drive for rapid change would not have been so thorough, and one must doubt if steam could have been banished by 1968 under such a regime. But would the railways still have been able to recruit staff to work in the dirty conditions that were a part of the steam scene? And with steam still dominant and costs thereby higher, might not some of the Beeching cuts have been even more severe? What is clear is that, as seen at the time, the right decisions were made in general. One can legitimately argue that the circumstances which led to short lives of BR standard steam and of some early diesels were not readily foreseeable. Indeed, when so much money for modernisation was made available by the Conservative government of the day, who was likely to turn down the offer?

Though the changes were certainly traumatic for many involved in them, one must surely conclude that the new era, which dawned with rail blue, the double-arrow and the end of steam, heralded the rebirth of the railways in Great Britain. From 1968 passenger traffic has actually climbed back to totals similar to those carried on the much larger BR system prior to the Beeching cuts. There is triumph in that, is there not?

Top right:
Stanier 'Black Five' No 45446 enters Shap cutting with an unbanked northbound fitted freight in July 1965. Colour-Rail BRM341/A. E. R. Cope

Bottom right:
The Scottish 'A4s' lost their gloss but were put to good use in their declining years. No 60006 *Sir Ralph Wedgwood* drifts down past Bridge of Allan with the up 'Grampian' in September 1964. Colour-Rail SC204/A. E. R. Cope

Above:
Polmadie depot in south Glasgow displays locomotives Nos 73072, 76104, 70035 and 45112 in July 1966, not long before the end of steam there.
Colour-Rail SC332/
K. C. H. Fairley

Right:
On the Waverley route near Hawick, Type 4 No D87 is seen with a down express heading towards Edinburgh.
Colour-Rail DE1006/
R. B. McCartney

Below right:
AEI/Metro-Vick ac electric Bo-Bo No E3048 heads south on the West Coast main line with an up express.
Colour-Rail DE711/D. Smith

Below:

In 1966 locomotives began to be painted in BR's new rail blue livery. A 350hp shunter, No D4100, was the first to emerge from Eastleigh works in these colours, and it displayed dark brown frames and wheels, a colour quickly replaced on locomotives by black. Colin Boocock

Bottom:

Express passenger EMUs on the Southern were first repainted rail blue in the new image, but they soon received the standard blue and grey as seen on 4-BIG unit No 7035 in 1967. Colin Boocock

Top:
Illustrative of the beginning of another era of piebald trains (ie of mixed liveries) is this view of 'Western' C-C diesel-hydraulic No D1067 *Western Druid* threading the 17.30 Bristol-Plymouth through the South Devon hills near Dainton summit, in July 1967. Colour-Rail DE581/P. W. Gray

Above:
By June 1968 delivery of the new Class 50 Co-Cos had reached No D421. This class were the last mixed traffic diesel locomotives to be built for British Rail.
Colour-Rail DE746/T. J. Edgington

Above:

'Black Five' 4-6-0 No 44680, one of eight fitted with Skefko roller bearings, hammers uphill through Ribblehead station towards Batty Moss viaduct with a northbound freight in April 1967. Colour-Rail BRM721/D. Smith

Below:

Expected at the time to be the final steam train to run on British Rail, the 'last steam special' of August 1968 climbs to Ais Gill summit double-headed by 'Black Fives' Nos 44871 and 44781. Crowds cheered, men wept, the last wisp faded into the atmosphere, and the steam age had ended.
Colour-Rail BRM102/R. Jones

As the sun begins to set on steam power on BR, a Stanier 'Black Five' 4-6-0 is seen with a diverted Crewe —Carlisle parcels train between Preston and Blackburn.
Colour-Rail BRM606/ M. Chapman

APPENDICES
The non-steam prototypes

The use of prototype locomotives usually has one of two objectives. Either a railway wishes to gain experience of a new form of traction, or a manufacturer wants to demonstrate the performance of a particular product. BR's first prototype non-steam locomotives were mostly aimed at gaining experience of new forms of traction. This certainly applied to the two LMS/English Electric Co-Cos, Nos 10000 and 10001, and to the three Southern diesel-electrics, Nos 10201-10203. The NBL/Paxman/BTH Bo-Bo diesel electric No 10800 was a useful machine for gaining experience of what a small, 827hp locomotive could do. Equally, the two Western Region gas-turbine locomotives were aimed at exploring the potential of a novel form of motive power. However, the 'Fell' diesel, the 2-D-2 four-engined diesel mechanical prototype, was so unusual as to be more of an experimental locomotive.

The most famous prototype appeared in 1955. The English Electric Napier 'Deltic' 3,300hp Co-Co was developed to demonstrate the potential for lightweight, high powered traction for high speed operation. It spent some time on the London Midland Region hauling such trains as the up 'Manxman', and was tested enthusiastically on the East Coast route. Its success led to the order for 22 Type 5s for that line. The 'Deltic' prototype is preserved in the Science Museum at South Kensington.

In 1961-62 manufacturers produced four prototypes to bid for the emerging market for higher powered traction in the 2,500-2,750hp range. Three diesel-electric designs appeared from Brush, BRCW and English Electric. All were Co-Cos, but there their similarities ended. Brush's

Falcon used two Maybach engines driving dc generators feeding power to the six traction motors. This was the only prototype eventually to form part of BR stock. BRCW's entry used the Sulzer 12LDA28A engine uprated to 2,750hp, which was similar to the unit used in the later Class 47. *Lion* was striking in its white livery. The English Electric Company produced No DP2 by using a 'Deltic'-style body and bogies and providing a 2,700hp version of its 16-cylinder engine. This was probably the most successful of the later diesel prototypes. All three locomotives were tested in two or more regions. *Lion's* withdrawal apparently occurred as a result of the financial difficulties of its parent company. DP2 was damaged beyond repair in an accident on the East Coast main line. *Falcon*, as No D1200, was withdrawn in 1975.

The oddest experimental machine was the GT3 gas-turbine mechanical locomotive which English Electric produced in 1962. It used a 2,700hp gas-turbine unit driving through mechanical gears to six-coupled axles. It was unidirectional, which was odd, and carried its fuel in a tender behind the cab in steam locomotive fashion. This interesting machine certainly worked, but BR's interest was in diesels and GT3 did not enter regular service.

The most powerful diesel locomotive ever to run in the United Kingdom was the Brush Co-Co known as *Kestrel*. Its Sulzer Vee-form engine delivered 4,000hp, essential for 125mph operation. Otherwise it was a conventional diesel-electric locomotive. Its axleload proved to be too heavy for very high speed work, though after acquiring new bogies it did perform useful work on the East Coast main line. Surprisingly, it was sold to Russia in 1971.

PROTOTYPE MAIN LINE LOCOMOTIVES ON BR

Builder	Number series	Rating (hp)	Engine type	Transmission	Wheel arrangement	Weight (tons)	Speed (mph)	Total built	Class (1968)
LMS/LMR	10000	1,600	EE	EE	Co-Co	122	90	2	—
SR	10201	1,750	EE	EE	1Co-Co1	135	90	2	—
SR	10203	2,000	EE	EE	1Co-Co1	132	90	1	—
Brown-Boveri	18000	2,500	Brown-Boveri gas-turbine	BBC	A1A-A1A	115	90	1	—
Metro-Vick	18100	3,000	Metro-Vick gas-turbine	Metro-Vick	Co-Co	130	90	1	—
BR	10100	2,000	Paxman (4)	Fell	2-D-2	120	72	1	—
NBL	10800	827	Paxman	BTH	Bo-Bo	70	70	1	—
SR	11001	500	Paxman	mechanical	0-6-0	49	c40	1	—
EE	Deltic	3,300	Napier Deltic (2)	EE	Co-Co	106	90	1	—
Brush	D0280	2,800	Maybach (2)	Brush	Co-Co	115	100	1	53
BRCW	D0260	2,750	Sulzer	AEI	Co-Co	114	100	1	—
EE	DP2	2,700	EE	EE	Co-Co	105	90	1	—
EE	GT3	2,700	EE gas-turbine	mechanical	2-C+3	85*	90	1	—
Brush	HS4000	4,000	Sulzer V	Brush	Co-Co	133	125	1	—

* Without fuel tender.

Top:

The two LMS-designed Co-Co diesel-electric prototypes, Nos 10000 and 10001, both spent a period working on the Southern Region as part of a five-strong fleet which included the three SR 1Co-Co1s. No 10000 heads the down 'Royal Wessex' near Shawford Junction, Winchester, in 1954. The train left Waterloo at 4.35pm and carried portions for Bournemouth West, Swanage and Weymouth.
Colour-Rail DE625/B. J. Swain

Above:

SR 2,000hp forerunner of the English Electric Type 4s, No 10203, had charge of the down 'Golden Arrow' Pullman boat train from Victoria to Dover near Petts Wood in March 1955. Colour-Rail DE631/S. C. Townroe

Top right:

Repainted in BR standard green, the Swiss-built Brown-Boveri A1A-A1A gas-turbine electric locomotive receives attention in August 1957 outside Swindon works.
Colour-Rail DE838/T. B. Owen

Bottom right:

The eclipse of two prototypes: the North British/Paxman/BTH 827hp Bo-Bo No 10800 stands stored at Derby works in November 1958. Beyond it the remains of the Fell diesel mechanical, by then changed to a 2-B-B-2, stand partially dismantled. Colour-Rail DE513/R. Bowyer

Above:
The prototype 3,300hp 'Deltic' heads up the East Coast main line with a southbound express in June 1959.
Colour-Rail DE574/
P. J. Hughes

Right:
The Brush/Maybach 2,800hp Co-Co No D0280 *Falcon* was private industry's first entry into the market for a more powerful Type 4 diesel, which culminated in the construction of the Class 47s. Here, *Falcon* is seen at Reading on an up express in July 1965.
Colour-Rail DE633/B. J. Swain

Below right:
D0260 *Lion* was the Birmingham Railway Carriage & Wagon Co's design for the required larger Type 4. It was fitted with a 12-cylinder 2,750hp Sulzer engine and AEI electrical equipment, and is seen here at King's Cross in September 1963.
Colour-Rail DE318/R. Hill

106

Above:
The oddest experiment of the 1960s was the rigid-framed gas-turbine mechanical locomotive No GT3, a product of English Electric. It was photographed climbing Shap bank with a test train in October 1961. Colour-Rail DE315/D. Cross

Below:
The English Electric Co built a conventional Co-Co with a 2,700hp 16-cylinder engine in a body based on that of the production 'Deltics'. Numbered DP2, it is seen calling at Rugby in 1962 while working the up 'Manxman'.
Colin Boocock

The last privately-offered main line prototype was the
Brush/Sulzer 4,000hp Co-Co *Kestrel*. It was built in 1968 at
the time when 125mph running was being considered by BR.
Seen at Crewe in its original condition, *Kestrel* later
received bogies similar to those fitted to the Brush Type 4s
(Class 47s) so that it could be run on BR at high speeds.
Colour-Rail DE695/M. Burnett

Livery styles on British Railways

On steam locomotives from mid-1948, four different liveries were adopted by British Railways as follows:

- Class 8P: Blue with black and white lining
- Classes 7P, 6P and 5P*: Brunswick green, with black and orange lining
- Mixed traffic engines, and Classes 4P down to 0P: Black with red, cream and grey lining
- Freight engines: Plain black

*Initially, however, the 'Schools' class 4-4-0s were lined black.

After a short time, the blue livery was replaced by Brunswick green. In the late 1950s and 1960s the exact distribution of the liveries and lining among the power groups was frequently changed.

Diesel and electric locomotives received liveries as follows:

- Main line: Black, with silver-grey line along mid-body, silver grey bogies
- Shunting: Plain black

Later, overall Brunswick green was used on all non-steam types, except on the Southern Region where stock green (similar to but darker than the former SR malachite) was applied to all its non-steam traction other than BRCW Type 3s and the standard 350hp shunting locomotives. Also, on the Western Region, Type 4 diesel-hydraulics were later repainted maroon, some of the 'Western' class receiving other experimental colours.

Non-steam locomotives received yellow warning panels on their cab fronts, initially small, but from 1966 extending over the whole cab front. Basic lettering styles and symbols used on all locomotives from 1948 to 1965 are illustrated in the accompanying photographs. All diesel and electric locomotives were repainted rail blue from 1965, at works overhauls.

Diesel and electric multiple units on the Southern were painted plain stock green from the early 1950s. On other Regions they were initially painted dark green, lined in cream, but many types later appeared in stock green, sometimes lined in cream. These were later often repainted dark green, not always lined out. The Clacton EMU sets were painted maroon, lined in black and cream. After 1965 all multiple units began to receive plain rail blue, except for the Clacton sets which were blue and grey. Progressively from 1967 other units were reliveried in blue and grey also.

From 1965, the earlier lettering styles and symbols were replaced with the new corporate identity lettering and the modern double-arrow motif. The new style was also applied to the Vale of Rheidol narrow gauge engines, but to no other steam locomotives.

Left:
The British Railways lion-over-wheel symbol of 1948 was a proud emblem to carry on a locomotive. Colin Boocock

Below:
From 1956 a new symbol was applied to all locomotives, incorporating the lion-holding-wheel-over-crown emblem from the British Transport Commission's new heraldic crest. The new double-arrow symbol was introduced in 1965 as a part of the campaign to establish a corporate image which would visually sever the link with the steam era. Colin Boocock

Right:
Locomotive numbers were displayed, like the standard lettering, in a simple, sans serif style. 'Princess' Pacific No 46203 *Princess Margaret Rose* carries the smaller size which was used when full lining would cause the larger size figures to appear cramped. Colin Boocock

Below right:
Locomotive nameplates were painted with black backgrounds under BR central policy from 1948, as is illustrated by this 1959 shot of 'Merchant Navy' Pacific No 35005. Unofficially, most of the main works eventually reverted to painting the much more popular red backgrounds (or blue in the case of the SR 'Battle of Britain' class). Colin Boocock

A 'danger' signal and the setting sun add to the atmosphere
of the approaching end of steam on British Rail as class '8F'
2-8-0 No 48206 hauls freight at Woodley in Greater
Manchester in that fateful year of 1968.
Colour-Rail BRM620/B. Magilton